D1611875

**Mc
Graw
Hill
Education**

Cover and Title Page: Nathan Love

www.mheonline.com/readingwonders

Send all inquiries to:
McGraw-Hill Education
2 Penn Plaza
New York, NY 10121

ISBN: 978-0-02-132618-1
MHID: 0-02-132618-5

Printed in the United States of America

1 2 3 4 5 6 7 8 9 QVS 20 19 18 17 16 15

A

ELD
Companion Worktext

Program Authors
Diane August
Jana Echevarria
Josefina V. Tinajero

Mc
Graw
Hill
Education

Unit 1

Friends and Family

The Big Idea

How do families and friends learn, grow,
and help one another?

(t) Marcin Piwowarski (c) Carol Walker/naturepl.com (b) hana/Datacraft/Getty Images

Animal Discoveries

The Big Idea

(t) Jeff Foott/Discovery Channel Images/Getty Images (c) Accent Alaska.com/Alamy (b) Susanne Danegger/Zoonar; D. Hurst/Alamy

Unit 3

Live and Learn

(t) Debby Tewa (c) Wave/Photolibrary (b) Bebeto Matthews/AP Images

Unit 4

Our Life, Our World

The Big Idea

Unit 5

Let's Make a Difference

(t) Daniel Griffo (b) Richard Johnson

Unit 6

How on Earth?

Friends and Family

The Big Idea

How do families and friends learn, grow, and help one another?

TALK ABOUT IT

? Essential Question
How do friends depend on each other?

>> *Go Digital*

14

What are the friends doing? Describe how they can help each other. When do we depend on friends? Write your ideas on the chart.

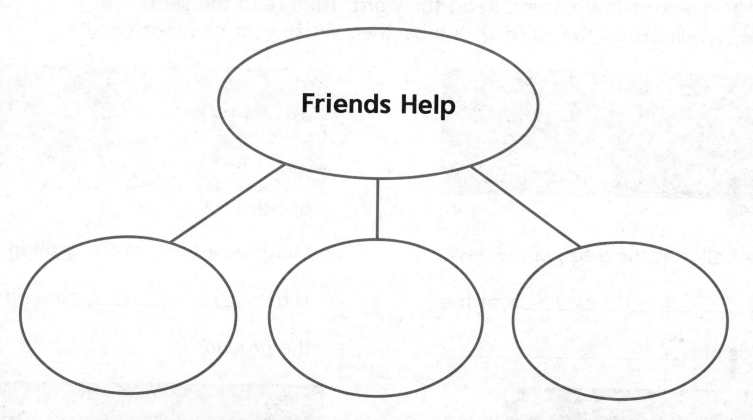

Friends Help

Talk about how friends depend on each other. Use the words from the chart. You can say:

Friends help _____

_____.

Friends depend on each other to _____

_____.

More Vocabulary

COLLABORATE Look at the picture. Read the word. Then read the sentence.
Talk about the word with a partner. Write your own sentence.

edge

The ball is at the **edge** of my desk.

My _____ is at the

edge of _____.

feelings

The friends have happy **feelings**.

People can have _____ or

_____ *feelings*.

ground

Many leaves are on the **ground**.

The _____ grows from

the *ground*.

lifted

Balloons **lifted** up into the air.

A _____ *lifts* into the

air when _____.

16

practice

They **practice** soccer together.

I *practice* _____

to _____.

uneasy

She felt **uneasy** about the ride.

Another word for *uneasy* is

_____.

Words and Phrases
Multiple-Meaning Words *get*

The word *get* can mean "go and take back."
Carlos gets a book from the library.

The word *get* can also mean "become."
The grass gets wet in the rain.

Read the sentences below. Circle the correct meaning for the word *get* in each sentence.

Sue <u>gets</u> her hat and coat.

goes and takes back   **becomes**

Did Dan <u>get</u> tired during the walk?

go and take back   **become**

» *Go Digital* **Add the two meanings for the word *get* to your New Words notebook. Write a sentence to show the meaning of each.**

COLLABORATE

1 Talk About It

Look at the picture. Read the title. Talk about what you see. Write your ideas.

What does the title tell you?

_____

_____

_____

What is the little bird doing?

_____

_____

_____

Take notes as you read the text.

Little Flap Learns to Fly

Essential Question

? How do friends depend on each other?

Read how Little Flap depends on his friends.

18

Little Flap was happy living in his nest. His friends, Fluff and Tuff, lived in the nest next to him. Every morning they sang songs **together**. Their parents brought them worms to eat.

One day Fluff asked, "Can we get our own worms?"

Tuff said, "We can if we learn to fly."

Fluff said, "Yes! Let's learn to fly."

① **Specific Vocabulary** Ⓐ Ⓒ Ⓣ

Reread the first paragraph. The word *together* means "with each other." Underline what the birds do together.

② **Sentence Structure** Ⓐ Ⓒ Ⓣ

Reread the second paragraph. Circle the words that tell you who speaks. Circle the punctuation mark that shows the character asks a question.

③ **Comprehension**
Key Details

Reread the rest of the page. Why does Fluff want to learn to fly?

Fluff wants to learn to fly

_____

_____.

19

Text Evidence 🔍

1 Comprehension

Key Details

Reread the first paragraph. Underline details that tell why Little Flap feels scared.

2 Sentence Structure Ⓐ Ⓒ Ⓣ

The word *so* connects two parts of the fifth sentence. Circle the part that tells why Little Flap keeps his feelings a secret.

3 Specific Vocabulary Ⓐ Ⓒ Ⓣ

The word *copied* means "did the same actions as someone else." What actions do Tuff and Little Flap copy?

They copy Fluff _____

_____

_____ .

Little Flap peered over the **edge** of his nest. It was very high up. When he looked down, the **ground** seemed very far away. He felt scared! He was too afraid to tell his friends about his fear so he kept his **feelings** a secret.

Fluff said, "Let's **practice** flapping our wings. It will make them strong. Watch."

Tuff and Little Flap watched Fluff. Then they **copied** her actions.

Soon it was time to fly. Little Flap could **no longer** keep his feelings a secret. He asked, "Will I fall? I don't want to get hurt."

Tuff said, "You can depend on Fluff and me. We're your friends."

Fluff said, "I have an idea. We will go first and show you how. Then you can try. If you fall, Tuff and I will rescue you."

Tuff said, "Yes, we can save you!" Tuff and Fluff jumped out of the nest. They flew!

Little Flap looked down nervously. He still felt **uneasy**, but he felt braver with his friends. "Okay," he said. "Let's try!"

Tim Beaumont

1 Specific Vocabulary ⒶⒸⓉ

Reread the second sentence. The words *no longer* tell about something Little Flap cannot do anymore. Circle what he can no longer do.

COLLABORATE

2 Talk About It

Talk about Fluff's idea. How do Fluff and Tuff help Little Flap learn to fly?

_____

_____

_____

3 Comprehension
Key Details

Reread the last paragraph. Underline the details that help you understand how Little Flap feels.

1 Sentence Structure Ⓐ Ⓒ Ⓣ

Reread the third sentence. Circle the word that connects the two actions the birds do together. Underline the words that tell about the actions.

2 Comprehension
Key Details

In the first paragraph, circle the detail that describes Little Flap flying.

3 Specific Vocabulary

When you do something *just right,* you make no mistakes. Circle a word with almost the same meaning as "just right." What is Little Flap doing just right?

Little Flap is _____

_____.

The three birds stood together on the branch. They counted, "One! Two! Three!" Then they flapped their wings fast and jumped. Little Flap **lifted** into the air.

"You're flying **just right**!" said Fluff.

"You're flying perfectly!" said Tuff.

All three little birds landed in a patch of soft, green grass.

Little Flap said, "Now I know I can always depend on you, Fluff and Tuff! You are my friends."

Then he found a big, juicy worm and shared it with his friends.

Now Little Flap likes flying!

Make Connections

? Describe how Little Flap depends on his friends. ESSENTIAL QUESTION

Discuss a time when you depended on your friends. TEXT TO SELF

Tim Beaumont

Text Evidence

1 **Comprehension**
Key Details

In the first sentence, underline the words that tell you the birds land safely.

2 **Sentence Structure** **A** **C** **T**

Reread the second paragraph. Box the names of the characters the pronoun *you* refers to. Underline what Little Flap says to the characters.

COLLABORATE

3 **Talk About It**

Talk about what Little Flap does when he finds a worm. How is Little Flap a good friend to Fluff and Tuff?

_____

_____.

Respond to the Text

Partner Discussion Answer the questions. Discuss what you learned about "Little Flap Learns to Fly." Write the page numbers where you found text evidence.

Why is Little Flap afraid?

The little birds want to fly because _____.

Page(s): _____

Little Flap looks down and _____.

Page(s): _____

Little Flap says _____.

Page(s): _____

How does Little Flap depend on his friends?

Text Evidence

Fluff shows how _____.

Page(s): _____

Fluff has an idea. She and Tuff _____.

Page(s): _____

If Little Flap falls, then _____.

Page(s): _____

Group Discussion Present your answers to the group. Cite text evidence to justify your thinking. Listen to and discuss the group's opinions about your ideas.

Write Review your notes. Then write your answer to the Essential Question. Use text evidence to support your answer. Use vocabulary words in your writing.

How does Little Flap depend on his friends?

Little Flap feels _____ because _____

_____. The little birds

_____ their wings. Fluff and Tuff

will go first, and _____

_____.

Little Flap depends on his friends _____

_____.

Share Writing Present your writing to the class. Discuss their opinions. Think about what the class has to say. Do they justify their claims? Explain why you agree or disagree.

I agree with _____ because _____.

I disagree because _____.

Write to Sources

Anita

Take Notes About the Text I took notes about the text on this chart to respond to the prompt: *Add to the story. Tell why Little Flap shares his worm with Fluff and Tuff.*

pages 18–23

Little Flap, Fluff, and Tuff want to get worms.

⬇

Little Flap is scared, but his friends help him to fly.

⬇

Little Flaps finds a big, juicy worm.

⬇

Little Flap wants to share because his friends helped him.

Write About the Text I used my notes to write about Little Flap sharing the worm.

Little Flap flew! Now he wanted to do something nice for Fluff and Tuff. Little Flap found a big, juicy worm. Fluff and Tuff looked hungry. It was lunchtime. Little Flap wanted to share his worm. Little Flap cut the worm into three pieces. The friends ate lunch.

TALK ABOUT IT

COLLABORATE

Text Evidence **Underline** the sentence that tells what Little Flap finds. Does the sentence add a descriptive detail?

Grammar **Circle** the word that tells how many. Why did Anita use a number word to tell how Little Flap cuts the worm?

Connect Ideas **Draw a box** around the sentence that tells how Fluff and Tuff look. What word can you use to connect it with the next sentence?

Your Turn

COLLABORATE

Add to the story. Have Fluff tell a new friend how he taught Little Flap to fly.

>> *Go Digital*
Write your response online. Use your editing checklist.

TALK ABOUT IT

Weekly Concept Families Around the World

? Essential Question
How are families around the world the same and different?

>> *Go Digital*

28

COLLABORATE

How does this family celebrate the spring season? Write on the chart how family celebrations are the same and how they can be different.

Same	Different

Discuss how family celebrations are the same and how they can be different. Use the words from the chart. Complete the sentences

Around the world, all families _____

_____

Families have different _____

_____.

More Vocabulary

Look at the picture. Read the word. Then read the sentence. Talk about the word with a partner. Write your own sentence.

chance

He has a **chance** to share ideas.

Another word for *chance* is

_____.

hurrying

We are **hurrying** to class.

I am *hurrying* when I need to

_____.

line

We **line** the street for the parade.

We *line* the soccer field to _____

_____.

proud

Dad is **proud** of me for helping.

I feel *proud* when I _____

_____.

sparkling

The ice is **sparkling** with light.

Another word for *sparkling* is

_____.

surprised

Jane is **surprised** by the news.

I was *surprised* when _____

_____.

(t) Melissa Fague/Monument Open/Getty Images; (b) Ingram Publishing

Words and Phrases
make and *make your way*

make = to build or create
She <u>makes</u> a birthday card for a friend.

make your way = start to go somewhere
We need to <u>make our way</u> to class.

Read the sentences below. Replace the underlined words with the correct form of "make" or "make your way" to complete each sentence.

She <u>builds</u> sand castles at the beach.

She _____ sand castles at the beach.

The students <u>start to go</u> back inside school.

The students _____
back inside school.

>> Go Digital Add *make* and *make your way* to your New Words notebook. Write a sentence to show the meaning of each.

COLLABORATE

1 Talk About It

Look at the pictures. Read the title. Talk about what you see. Write your ideas.

What does this title tell you?

_____

_____

_____.

What is the girl in the picture doing?

_____

_____

_____.

Take notes as you read the text.

Maria Celebrates Brazil

Essential Question

? How are families around the world the same and different?

Read about a family from Brazil.

Maria and her family are in their bright, hot kitchen. "Please, Mãe, por favor!" Maria begs.

Mãe speaks **Portuguese**. This is the language of Brazil. "No matter how much you beg or plead, you must go to practice. The parade is next week."

1 Sentence Structure A C T

Circle the comma in the first sentence. Box the two adjectives that describe the family's kitchen.

2 Specific Vocabulary A C T

Reread the second paragraph. Underline the sentence that tells about the word *Portuguese*.

3 Comprehension
Character, Setting, Events

Explain what Maria must do.

She must go to _____

because _____

is next week.

Janet Broxon

33

Text Evidence

1 Specific Vocabulary ⒶⒸⓉ

Reread the second paragraph. The words *do the right thing* mean "do the correct or good thing." What is the right thing for Maria to do? Underline the words that tell you.

2 Sentence Structure ⒶⒸⓉ

Reread the first and second sentences of the last paragraph. Circle the noun that the pronoun *it* refers to.

COLLABORATE

3 Talk About It

Discuss why Pai says the parade is important. Then write about it.

_____

_____

_____.

34

"It's not fair," says Maria in English.

Mãe does not know a lot of English. Maria is **surprised** when she asks, "What is not fair about going to practice? You must **do the right thing**."

"Ana invited me to her house," Maria answers. "I want to go!"

Pai says, "Maria, the parade is important. People from around the world come to see it. They try our food, see how we dress, and how we live. It is a **chance** for us to share our culture."

"I know but I really want to see Ana," says Maria.

Pai says, "Maria, you can see Ana another time. They are giving out costumes at practice today."

Maria thinks about her father's words. Pai is right. She and the other children have worked hard for a year. They practiced their dance steps over and over. They even made their own bright colorful costumes.

Text Evidence

1 Sentence Structure A C T

Reread the first paragraph. Circle the words that show that Maria is speaking. Underline what Maria says she wants to do.

2 Comprehension
Character, Setting, Events

Reread the second paragraph. Underline the important detail about practice today.

COLLABORATE

3 Talk About It

Why does Maria know her father, Pai, is right?

_____

_____

_____

35

Text Evidence

1 **Comprehension**
Character, Setting, Events

In the second paragraph, circle details that tell when and where the story event takes place.

2 **Sentence Structure**

Reread the third sentence in the second paragraph. Box the words in the subject. Underline what the people are doing.

COLLABORATE

3 **Talk About It**

Discuss why it was important for Maria and her group to practice. What do they know how to do?

_____

_____

_____.

36

"You're right," Maria says to her father. "I'll go to practice. I'll tell Ana I cannot visit her."

One week passes. Lots of people **line** the streets. The children in Maria's group are wearing their **sparkling** costumes. They know each dance step. They dance to the beat.

The crowd moves aside as they make their way down the street.

When the crowd moves away, Maria sees a woman with a camera. She is **hurrying**. The woman scurries by Maria. She puts her camera to her eye. Maria **smiles from ear to ear**. She is excited to be in the parade. Click! The woman takes a picture of Maria. Maria is **proud** of her hard work!

Make Connections

? How is Maria's family the same and different from other families you know? ESSENTIAL QUESTION

Compare Maria's family to your own family. TEXT TO SELF

Janet Broxon

1 Sentence Structure Ⓐ Ⓒ Ⓣ

Reread the first sentence in the second paragraph. Circle the comma that shows the sentence has two parts. Underline what happens when the crowd moves away.

2 Specific Vocabulary Ⓐ Ⓒ Ⓣ

The words *smiles from ear to ear* mean "makes a big, wide smile." In the second paragraph, circle why Maria smiles from ear to ear.

COLLABORATE

3 Talk About It

How does Maria feel during the parade?

_____

_____

_____.

37

Respond to the Text

Partner Discussion Answer the questions. Discuss what you learned about "Maria Celebrates Brazil." Write the page numbers where you found text evidence.

Why is the parade important to Maria's family?

Mãe and Pai want Maria to _____.

Pai says the parade is important because _____.

Maria and the other children _____.

Text Evidence 🔍

Page(s): _____

Page(s): _____

Page(s): _____

What happens at the parade?

Many people line _____.

Maria's group wears their costumes and _____.

At the end of the story, Maria feels _____.

Text Evidence 🔍

Page(s): _____

Page(s): _____

Page(s): _____

Group Discussion Present your answers to the group. Cite text evidence to justify your thinking. Listen to and discuss the group's opinions about your answers.

Write Review your notes. Then write your answer to the Essential Question. Use text evidence to support your answer. Use vocabulary words in your writing.

How does Maria help celebrate the culture of Brazil?

Maria understands that the parade is important because

_____

_____.

Maria and the other children _____

_____.

In the end, Maria is excited to _____

and feels _____.

Share Writing Present your writing to the class. Discuss their opinions. Think about what the class has to say. Do they justify their claims? Explain why you agree or disagree.

I agree with _____ because _____. I disagree because _____.

Write to Sources

Alex

Maria Celebrates Brazil

pages 32–37

Take Notes About the Text I took notes on this idea web to respond to the prompt: *Write a paragraph. Describe the costume Maria makes.*

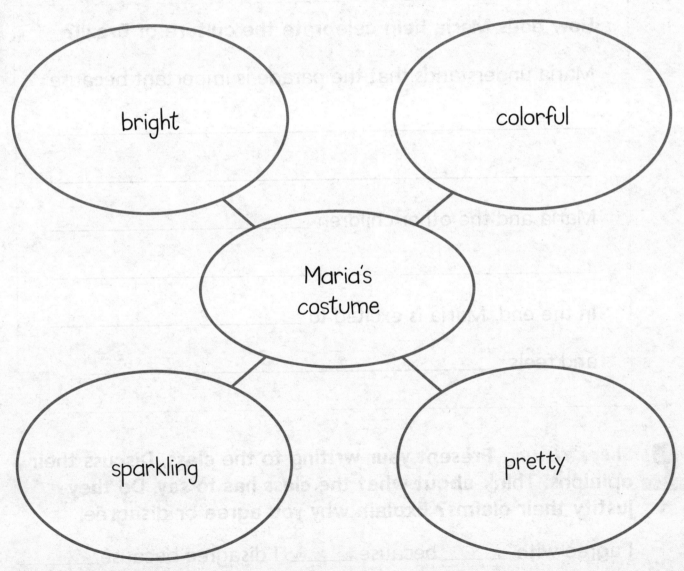

- bright
- colorful
- Maria's costume
- sparkling
- pretty

40

Write About the Text I used my notes to write a paragraph with descriptive details about Maria's costume.

Maria makes a colorful costume for the parade. She wears purple feathers on her head. There are pink feathers, too. Her costume has a white and gold skirt. It is bright and sparkling. Maria looks like a pretty dancing bird!

TALK ABOUT IT

COLLABORATE

Text Evidence **Box** descriptive words from the notes. What other descriptive details did Alex use?

Grammar **Circle** the phrase that tells why Maria makes a colorful costume.

Condense Ideas **Underline** the sentences that tell about the feathers. How can you combine the sentences?

Your Turn

COLLABORATE

Think about the parade. Use details in the text to describe the parade in a paragraph.

>> Go Digital
Write your response online. Use your editing checklist.

Essential Question

How can a pet be an important friend?

>> *Go Digital*

42

COLLABORATE

What pet do you see? How is this pet a friend to the boy? Write on the chart some ways that pets can be important friends.

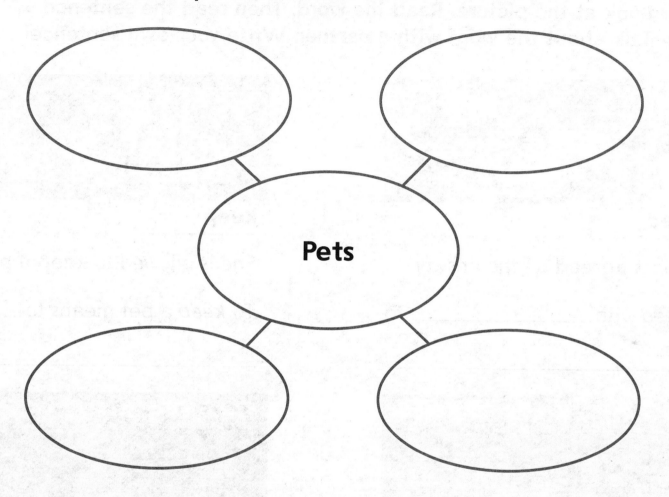

Pets

Discuss ways that pets can be our friends. Use the words from the chart. You can say:

Pets can _____ because they _____. Pets can

_____, and they _____.

More Vocabulary

COLLABORATE

Look at the picture. Read the word. Then read the sentence. Talk about the word with a partner. Write your own sentence.

agreed

The class **agreed** on the answer.

I *agreed* with _____ to

_____.

keep

She is allowed to **keep** a pet.

To *keep* a pet means to _____

_____.

connection

Mom and pup have a **connection**.

I have *connections* to _____

_____.

scratched

The cat **scratched** its ear.

I *scratched* my arm when _____

_____.

shelter

The dog stays at the **shelter**.

Animals _____

_____ at a *shelter*.

wiry

This grass feels **wiry**.

The opposite of *wiry* is

_____ .

take = need an amount of time
Dad <u>took</u> a long time to decide.

take = bring or carry
We <u>took</u> our dog to the park.

Read the sentences below. Circle the correct meaning of *take* in each sentence.

Maria <u>took</u> five minutes to walk home.

needed   **brought**

Dad <u>takes</u> me to see a movie.

needs   **brings**

>> *Go Digital* **Add the two meanings for the word *take* to your New Words notebook. Write a sentence to show each meaning of *take*.**

COLLABORATE

1 Talk About It

Look at the pictures. Read the title. Talk about what you see. Write your ideas.

What does this title tell

you? _____

_____

_____.

What is the boy doing?

_____

_____

_____.

Take notes as you read the text.

Finding Cal

Essential Question

?

How can a pet be an important friend?

Read about a dog who becomes a boy's special friend.

Dear Diary,

It took Dad a long time to decide. He finally **made up his mind**. Dad came to my room tonight. He said I could get a dog! But it has to be a small or medium-sized dog. We will go to the animal **shelter** tomorrow.

Medium Dog

Small Dog

Marcin Piwowarski

❶ Specific Vocabulary A C T

Circle the word in the first sentence that helps you understand the meaning of *made up his mind*.

❷ Sentence Structure A C T

An exclamation point shows a writer feels a strong way. Circle the exclamation point in the paragraph. Underline what the boy feels very happy about.

COLLABORATE

❸ Talk About It

Talk about what kind, or size, of dog Jake can get. Then write about it.

_____

_____

_____.

47

❶ Comprehension
Character, Setting, Events

Reread the first paragraph. Where are the characters now? Underline the words that tell the setting.

❷ Sentence Structure ⒶⒸⓉ

Reread the first sentence in the second paragraph. Circle the word that connects the two people. What is the subject in this sentence?

_____

❸ Specific Vocabulary ⒶⒸⓉ

Reread the rest of the paragraph. Find and circle a word that helps you understand the phrase *looking right at.* Who is looking right at Jake?

_____

Dear Diary,   September 26

Wow! There are so many different dogs at the shelter. There are big and little dogs. Some have soft fur and some have **wiry** hair.

Dad and I walked to one dog's cage. The tag said the dog's name was Cal. One quick glance at the cute dog, and I knew he was for me. Dad said, "Look, Jake! Look at how Cal stares at you." It was true! His eyes were wide open. He was **looking right at** me.

Jack   Spot   Sam   Cal

We put Cal on a leash and took him to a fenced yard. Cal smiled and stared at me. Cal wanted to play. In minutes he learned the proper, or correct, way to sit. He could walk on a leash nicely, too. I patted him on the head, and he licked my hand.

Cal licking my hand!

1 **Comprehension**
Character, Setting, Events

Reread the first sentence. Circle the details that tell about the change in setting.

2 **Sentence Structure**

Look back at the second sentence. What is the name of the character that the pronoun *me* refers to?

_____

COLLABORATE

3 **Talk About It**

Talk about what Cal learns. Then write about it.

_____

_____

_____

_____

Marcin Piwowarski

Text Evidence 🔍

① Comprehension
Character, Setting, Events

Read the first paragraph. Circle who sees a connection between Jake and Cal. Underline the sentence that states what Jake agrees with.

COLLABORATE

② Talk About It

What does Jake do to make

Cal feel better? _____

_____

_____.

③ Specific Vocabulary ACT

Reread the last paragraph. The words *a while* mean "a long time." Circle what Jake did not do in a while. Underline what Cal learned.

Dad said, "I see a real **connection** between you and Cal." I **agreed**. We already had a good relationship.

Soon we were on our way home. Cal was nervous so I tried to make him feel better. I **scratched** his ears, and he liked it.

Dear Diary, October 10

It has been **a while** since I have written. Cal has learned many new tricks like how to roll over. I have learned from Cal, too.

Cal's Tricks!

Cal walks with Dad and me to school every day. Each night, Dad reads me a story. Cal lies next to me. I would not trade him for any other dog. I will **keep** him because our friendship is very special. Finding Cal was worth the wait!

Make Connections

? How is Cal an important friend to Jake? ESSENTIAL QUESTION

Compare Jake's pet Cal to your pet or a pet you know. Tell how each pet is a good friend. TEXT TO SELF

Marcin Piwowarski

1 **Sentence Structure** Ⓐ Ⓒ Ⓣ

Reread the first sentence. Circle the subject. Underline the words that tell what the subject does.

2 **Comprehension**
Character, Setting, Events

Box the two sentences that describe what happens each night.

COLLABORATE

3 **Talk About It**

Why does Jake say he will not trade Cal for any other dog?

_____

_____

_____

_____.

51

Respond to the Text

Partner Discussion Answer the questions. Discuss what you learned about "Finding Cal." Write the page numbers where you found text evidence.

How does Jake find Cal?	Text Evidence 🔍
Dad said that Jake can _____.	Page(s): _____
At the _____, Dad and Jake _____.	Page(s): _____
Dad sees _____ between Jake and Cal.	Page(s): _____

Why do Cal and Jake have a special friendship?	Text Evidence 🔍
Cal learns new _____. Jake says he _____ from Cal.	Page(s): _____
Cal and Dad walk _____.	Page(s): _____
Each night, Cal _____ when _____.	Page(s): _____

Group Discussion Present your answers to the group. Cite text evidence to justify your thinking. Listen to and discuss the group's opinions about your answers.

Write Review your notes. Then write your answer to the Essential Question. Use text evidence to support your answer. Use vocabulary words in your writing.

How is Cal an important friend to Jake?

Dad and Jake find Cal _____.

Dad says he sees a _____.

between Cal and Jake. Jake teaches _____

_____.

Every day, _____.

Each night, _____.

Jake and Cal have _____.

Share Writing Present your writing to the class. Discuss their opinions. Think about what the class has to say. Did they justify their claims? Explain why you agree or disagree.

I agree with _____ because _____. I disagree because _____.

53

Write to Sources

James

Take Notes About the Text I took notes on this chart to respond to the prompt: *Add a diary entry about Jake teaching Cal a trick.*

pages 46–51

Dad says Jake can get a dog. Jake finds Cal.

↓

Cal learns to sit. Cal can walk on a leash.

↓

Cal learns new tricks. He can roll over.

↓

Cal walks to school with Jake. Cal sleeps with Jake. Jake and Cal have a special friendship.

Write About the Text **I used my notes to write a diary entry about teaching Cal a new trick.**

Student Model: *Narrative Text*

October 15

Dear Diary,

Cal is so smart! He can sit and roll over. I am teaching him a new trick. I put out my hand. I say, "Shake." Cal thinks about the trick. Cal puts his paw in my hand, and we shake! We have a special friendship.

TALK ABOUT IT

Text Evidence **Circle** details that come from the notes. Why did James include those details in his diary entry?

Grammar **Draw a box** around the word that connects two actions in the second sentence. What are the actions?

Connect Ideas **Underline** the sentences that tell what Jake does in the new trick. What word can be used to combine the two sentences?

Your Turn

Add a diary entry to the beginning of the story. Write about the time Jake and Dad talk about dogs.

>> Go Digital
Write your response online. Use your editing checklist.

55

TALK ABOUT IT

Weekly Concept Animals Need Care

? Essential Question

How do we care for animals?

>> *Go Digital*

What is the animal doing? How do people care for this animal? Write on the chart how we care for animals.

COLLABORATE

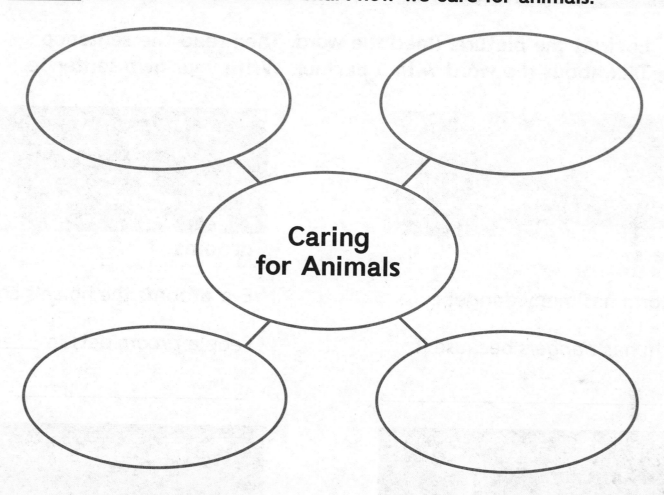

Caring
for Animals

Discuss ways people care for animals. Use the words from the chart. You can say:

People care for animals by _____

_____.

People give animals _____.

More Vocabulary

COLLABORATE Look at the picture. Read the word. Then read the sentence. Talk about the word with a partner. Write your own sentence.

dangers

The storm has many **dangers**.

A storm has *dangers* because it

_____.

grooms

Eva **grooms** the horse's coat.

People *groom* pets to _____

_____.

exercise

Good **exercise** keeps us healthy.

My favorite kind of *exercise* is

_____.

nature

Wild animals are part of **nature**.

Some animals I saw in *nature* are

_____.

refills

Kim **refills** the water every day.

The word *refills* means _____

_____ again.

shovels

Chris **shovels** the snow.

Chris *shovels* snow _____

_____ .

Words and Phrases
work, worked up

worked up = excited
The kids got <u>worked up</u> to see the movie.

<u>work</u> = a job or task to do
Tony cleans his bedroom and does other <u>work</u> at home.

Read the sentences below. Write *work* or *worked up* for the underlined words.

We finished the <u>job</u> Mom asked us to do.

We finished the _____ Mom asked us to do.

We got <u>excited</u> when we won the contest.

We got _____ when we won the contest.

>> Go Digital **Add *work* and *worked up* to your New Words notebook. Write a sentence to show the meaning of each.**

COLLABORATE

1 Talk About It

Look at the pictures. Read the title. Talk about what you see. Write your ideas.

What does this title tell you?

_____

_____

_____.

What is the boy doing with the horse?

_____

_____.

Take notes as you read the text.

Taking Care of Pepper

Essential Question

?

How do we care for animals?

Read about how a boy cares for a horse.

tbkgd) ©iStockphoto.com/nancykennedy

Have you ever been on a farm? Jack lives on a farm. He has a horse named Pepper. Jack helps take care of Pepper. **Looking after** a horse is a big job. A horse has many needs. There are a lot of things a horse must have to live.

① Sentence Structure Ⓐ Ⓒ Ⓣ

Read the second and third sentences. The pronoun *he* refers to a person. Circle the name of the boy who has a horse.

② Specific Vocabulary

Reread the rest of the page. In the fourth sentence, underline the words with the same meaning as *looking after*. Why is looking after a horse a big job?

_____

_____

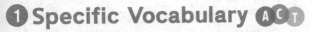

Text Evidence

1 Specific Vocabulary (A)(C)(T)

Reread the first paragraph. A *stall* is a horse's shelter, or home. Underline why Pepper has a stall.

2 Comprehension

Key Details

Reread the second paragraph and look back at the photo caption. Circle what Pepper does when he is excited to see Jack.

3 Sentence Structure (A)(C)(T)

Reread the second sentence in the last paragraph. The word *while* shows that two things happen at the same time. Underline the two things that happen at the same time.

Pepper stomps his hoof and nods his head when he sees Jack.

Every morning, Jack wakes up at 5:00 a.m. He and his father go to Pepper's **stall**. The stall keeps Pepper safe from bad weather and other **dangers**.

When Pepper sees Jack, the horse gets excited. Jack smiles when the horse gets all worked up.

First, Jack gives Pepper hay to eat. While Pepper eats, Jack cleans Pepper's stall. He **shovels** out the dirty hay and sawdust. Then he puts down fresh padding.

Tom Joslyn/Alamy

Next, Jack **strokes** Pepper's brown coat and it feels smooth. Then Jack leaves to go to school. But his work is not done!

At 3:00 p.m., Jack rides the bus back home. He has a snack and does his homework. Next, his mother gives him an apple for Pepper. Then they go to visit Pepper.

Jack feeds Pepper hay and fresh water every day.

Andy Crawford and Kit Houghton/Getty Images

❶ Specific Vocabulary Ⓐ Ⓒ Ⓣ

The verb *to stroke* has almost the same meaning as the verb *to pet*. Box what Jack strokes. Box the word that tells how it feels.

❷ Comprehension
Key Details

Reread the last paragraph. Circle what Jack does at 3:00 p.m. Underline the sentence that tells what he does when he gets home.

COLLABORATE

❸ Talk About It

Discuss what happens next in Jack's day. What will Jack do with the apple?

_____

_____.

63

1 Comprehension

Key Details

Reread the first three sentences. Underline the words that tell what Pepper can do in the field.

2 Sentence Structure A C T

Reread the fifth sentence. The predicate of the sentence is "made Pepper thirsty." Underline all the words in the subject.

COLLABORATE

3 Talk About It

Discuss Pepper's exercise. Why must Jack make sure Pepper gets exercise?

_____

_____

_____.

Jack and his mom find Pepper in a field. Pepper is allowed to roam. He can walk all around the field. He was drinking after having wandered the field. All that walking here and there made Pepper thirsty!

Now it is time for Pepper's **exercise**. In the wild, horses run many hours a day. But Pepper does not live out in **nature**. Jack must make sure Pepper gets the exercise he needs.

Pepper must have exercise each day.

Carol Walker/naturepl.com

Jack puts the **saddle** on Pepper. He places the bit in Pepper's mouth. Mom does the same thing with her horse, and they ride horses together.

When they are finished riding, Jack **grooms** Pepper. He brushes his mane, tail, and fur.

Finally, Jack gives Pepper more hay and **refills** his water bucket. "See you in the morning," Jack says. Pepper nods his head as if to say, "Yes, I'll be waiting!"

Jack's Dad checks for rocks in Pepper's hooves. If he sees one, he must get it out.

Make Connections

How do people care for horses? ESSENTIAL QUESTION

Compare the needs of a horse and another pet you know. Which needs more care? TEXT TO SELF

Text Evidence

1 Specific Vocabulary ACT

A *saddle* is a seat you put on a horse. Box the detail in the first paragraph that tells why Jack and Mom put saddles on their horses.

2 Comprehension
Key Details

Jack grooms Pepper. Circle each part of the horse that Jack brushes.

COLLABORATE

3 Talk About It

What happens at the end of Pepper's day?

_____

_____

_____.

Respond to the Text

Partner Discussion Answer the questions. Discuss what you learned from "Taking Care of Pepper." Write the page numbers where you found text evidence.

What is Jack's big job?

Text Evidence

Jack lives on a _____ and takes care of _____. Page(s): _____

A horse has many _____. Page(s): _____

One thing Jack does is shovel _____. Page(s): _____

What does Pepper need from Jack?

Text Evidence

Jack feeds Pepper _____. Page(s): _____

Jack makes sure Pepper runs because _____. Page(s): _____

Jack needs to groom Pepper and brush _____. Page(s): _____

Group Discussion Present your answers to the group. Cite text evidence to justify your thinking. Listen to and discuss the group's opinions about your answers.

66

Write Review your notes. Then write your answer to the Essential Question. Use text evidence to support your answer. Use vocabulary words in your writing.

What are some ways that Jack takes are of Pepper?

Jack feeds Pepper _____ and _____

his water bucket. Jack also _____ dirty hay and

sawdust. Jack makes sure Pepper _____

because Pepper _____.

Jack also grooms Pepper. Jack brushes _____

_____.

Share Writing Present your writing to the class. Discuss their opinions. Think about what the class has to say. Do they justify their claims? Explain why you agree or disagree with their claims.

I agree with _____ because _____.

I disagree because _____.

Write to Sources

pages 60–65

Sophie

Take Notes About the Text I took notes on the idea web to answer the questions:
Is taking care of a horse easy or hard?
Why do you think so?

taking care of a horse

Jack cleans dirty hay and sawdust from Pepper's stall.

Jack gives Pepper hay and water.

Jack rides Pepper. Then he brushes Pepper.

Write About the Text I used my notes to write
my opinion about taking care of a horse.

Student Model: *Opinion*

I think taking care of a horse
is hard. In the morning, Jack
feeds Pepper. He also has to clean
Pepper's stall. Later, he brushes
Pepper and gives him hay and
water. This is a lot of hard work!

TALK ABOUT IT

Text Evidence **Underline** the third sentence. What details from the idea web can be added to the sentence?

Grammar **Box** the phrase in the second sentence that tells when Jack feeds Pepper. What else does Jack do then?

Connect Ideas **Circle** the word Sophie uses to connect two actions. What two actions does the word connect?

Your Turn

Could you take care of a horse? Use details from the text in your answer.

>> Go Digital
Write your response online. Use your editing checklist.

69

? **Essential Question**
What happens when
families work together?

>> *Go Digital*

COLLABORATE

Describe what the family members are doing. How do families work together? Write your ideas on the chart.

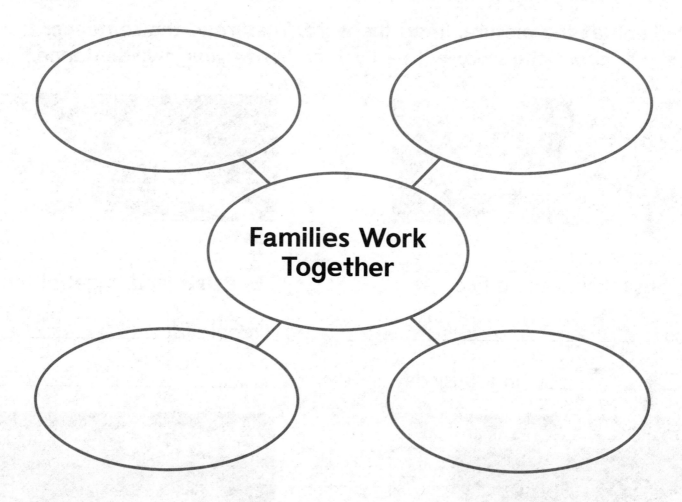

Families Work Together

Discuss ways a family can work together. Use the words from the chart. You can say:

A family works _____.

A family can _____.

More Vocabulary

COLLABORATE

Look at the picture. Read the word. Then read the sentence.
Talk about the word with a partner. Write your own sentence.

busy

It is a **busy** day at this office.

You do _____

_____ in a *busy* day.

future

I will learn to sing in the **future**.

In the *future*, I want to_____

_____.

lists

Dad **lists** food to get at the store.

People *list* _____

_____.

save

I **save** some money for later.

I *save* money when I _____

_____.

72

wants

The green bike is a **want** for Sam.

The bike is a *want* because _____

_____.

weekly

Dad does his **weekly** chore.

A *weekly* chore will happen

_____.

Words and Phrases
that

The word *that* is used in different ways.

To connect two parts of a sentence:
I found out <u>that</u> my cousin will visit.

To refer to something you already said:
Jake scored a goal. We needed <u>that</u> goal to win.

Read the sentence. Complete your own sentence using *that* in the same way.

I learned <u>that</u> our class has a field trip.

I learned _____.

Dad built a tree house. We used <u>that</u> tree house for our club.

We had free time. We used _____

_____.

>> Go Digital Add the word *that* to your New Words notebook. Write sentences to show the different uses of the word.

1 Talk About It

Look at the photographs. Read the title. Talk about what you see. Write your ideas.

What does this title tell you?

_____

_____

_____.

What is the doctor doing?

_____

_____

_____.

Take notes as you read the text.

Essential Question

? **What happens when families work together?**

Read about how one family works to meet their needs.

Masterfile.

74

Families Work!

Ellen Yung had a **busy** day at work! She put a cast on a broken arm, used a **bandage** to cover a deep cut, and helped twenty patients. Ellen is a doctor for children. Customers can get sick at any time, so pediatricians work long hours. They have hard jobs.

Ellen's husband works long hours, too. Steve is a firefighter. At the fire house, he makes sure the tools work properly. He checks the hoses and fire trucks. At the fire, Steve rescues people from hot flames and smoke. The firefighters all work together to put out the fire.

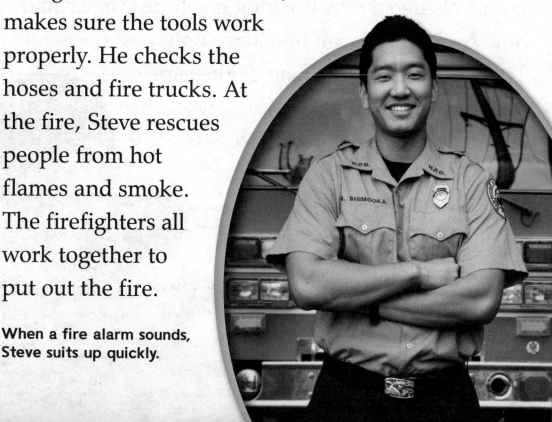

When a fire alarm sounds, Steve suits up quickly.

PBNJ Productions/Blend Images/Getty Images

❶ Specific Vocabulary ACT

Reread the second sentence. Underline a clue that helps you understand the meaning of *bandage*.

❷ Sentence Structure ACT

Reread the fourth sentence. Circle the comma that shows the sentence has two parts. Circle the reason Ellen works long hours.

❸ Comprehension
Key Details

Reread the last paragraph. Why do firefighters have an important job?

_____

_____

_____

_____.

75

Text Evidence

COLLABORATE

1 Talk About It

Reread the first paragraph. Talk about how each family member works at home.

What does everyone have?

2 Specific Vocabulary A C T

Find the word *both*. The word *both* in this sentence means "the two things." Draw boxes around the two things that cost the same.

3 Comprehension
Key Details

Underline the detail that tells why the family needed a new washing machine.

At home, the Yung family works together too. Hanna sets the table for dinner. She also helps wash the dishes. Everyone has **weekly** chores. Mom and Hanna do the dusting and mopping. Dad and her brother, Zac, do the laundry. They wash, dry, and fold the clothes. Mom makes a shopping list each week. She **lists** items they need and things they want.

A short time ago, Zac wanted a new laptop. The family needed a new washing machine. They could only spend money on one item. **Both** cost the same. They had to choose. Clean clothes are needed for school and work. A new laptop is nice, but did Zac need it? Ellen and Steve thought about their family's needs. They decided to buy the washing machine.

Hanna's brother, Zac, helps with the meals.

(t) hana/Datacraft/imagenavi/Getty Images; (b) MIXA next/Getty Images

76

What Are Some Needs and Wants?

Needs	Wants
Water	Skateboard
Food	Video game
Shelter	Basketball
Clothing	

Zac knows that his parents have busy jobs. They bring home money to pay for their needs and **wants**. They needed that washing machine. Zac still wants a laptop. The family has decided to **save** some money each week so they can buy it in the **future**.

Make Connections

? How does the Yung family work together? ESSENTIAL QUESTION

How is your family similar or different from the family in the story? TEXT TO SELF

Text Evidence

1 Sentence Structure Ⓐ Ⓒ Ⓣ

Reread the first two sentences. Circle the words *they* refers to. Underline why they bring home money.

2 Comprehension
Key Details

What will the family buy in the future?

_____

Circle the detail that tells how they can buy it.

COLLABORATE

3 Talk About It

Talk about the needs and wants in the chart. Why is food a need? Why is a video game a want?

77

(l) McGraw-Hill Companies, Inc. Ken Karp, Photographer; (r) C Squared Studios/Getty Images

Respond to the Text

Partner Discussion **Answer the questions. Discuss what you learned about "Families Work!" Write the page numbers where you found text evidence.**

How does each member of the Yung family work?

Ellen Yung _____.

Steve Yung _____.

At home, _____.

Text Evidence 🔍

Page(s): _____

Page(s): _____

Page(s): _____

How does the family decide what to buy?

The family has only enough _____.

They think about _____.

They buy the washing machine because _____.

Text Evidence 🔍

Page(s): _____

Page(s): _____

Page(s): _____

Group Discussion **Present your answers to the group. Cite text evidence to justify your thinking. Listen to and discuss the group's opinions about your answers.**

Write Review your notes. Then write your answer to the
Essential Question. Use text evidence to support your answer.
Use vocabulary words in your writing.

> **What happens when the Yung family works together?**
>
> Ellen and Steve Yung have busy jobs so they can _____
>
> _____.
>
> At home, the family works together, too. Zac and Dad
>
> _____.
>
> Mom and Hanna do _____.
>
> The family can buy the _____ they need
>
> and _____ to buy the laptop they want.

Share Writing Present your writing to the class. Discuss their
opinions. Think about what the class has to say. Do they
justify their claims? Explain why you agree or disagree.

I agree with _____ because _____. I disagree because _____.

Write to Sources

pages 74–77

Take Notes About the Text I took notes about the text and the "Wants and Needs" chart. Then I answered the question: *What does the chart tell about what families need?*

Lee

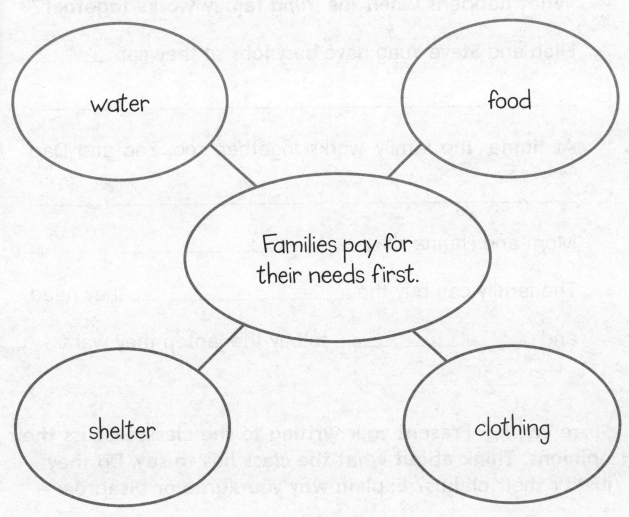

water

food

Families pay for their needs first.

shelter

clothing

Write About the Text I used my notes to write about what families need.

In the "Needs" part of the chart, the author tells what a family pays for first. The chart tells things every family needs to live. They need water, food, and shelter. They also need clothing. All families must have these things.

TALK ABOUT IT

Text Evidence Underline each *need* from Lee's web. Why did Lee include these details in his paragraph?

Grammar Box the comma in the first sentence. Where does the author tell what a family pays for first?

Connect Ideas Circle the commas in the third sentence. What are the three things in this sentence that families need?

Your Turn

What will the Yung family pay for first? Use details from the text in your answer.

>> Go Digital
Write your response online. Use your editing checklist.

Animal Discoveries

The Big Idea

How do animals play a part in the world around us?

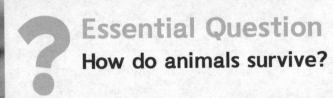

? Essential Question
How do animals survive?

>> *Go Digital*

Describe what the animals are doing in the picture. Write how animals survive on the chart.

COLLABORATE

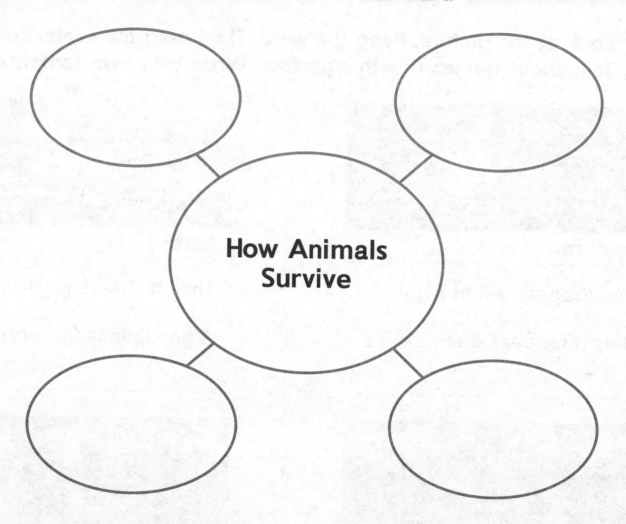

How Animals Survive

Discuss ways animals survive in nature. Use the words from the chart. You can say:

The animals _____ so

they _____.

85

More Vocabulary

Look at the picture. Read the word. Then read the sentence. Talk about the word with a partner. Write your own sentence.

disappeared

The sun **disappeared** at night.

The stars *disappear* when _____

_____.

explained

Kay **explained** the game.

When something is *explained*, you

_____ it.

hike

The children enjoyed the **hike**.

A good place for a *hike* is _____

_____.

hunt

Some birds **hunt** for bugs in trees.

The word *hunt* means to _____

_____.

sighed

The boy **sighed** after he lost.

I *sighed* when _____

_____.

wondered

Karina **wonders** what is in the box.

To *wonder* means to _____

_____.

Words and Phrases
looking forward to and *look for*

looking forward to = happy or excited about

I am <u>looking forward to</u> our family trip.

look for = search for

Please help me <u>look for</u> my library book.

Read the sentences below. Circle the correct meaning for the underlined words in each sentence.

José <u>looks for</u> the ball he lost.

happy or excited about   searches for

Are you <u>looking forward to</u> third grade?

happy or excited about   searching for

>> Go Digital Add the words *looking forward to* and *look for* to your New Words notebook. Write a sentence to show the meaning of each.

COLLABORATE

❶ Talk About It

Look at the pictures. Read the title. Talk about what you see. Write your ideas.

What does the title tell you?

_____

_____

_____.

What does the picture of the desert show?

_____

_____

_____

Take notes as you read the text.

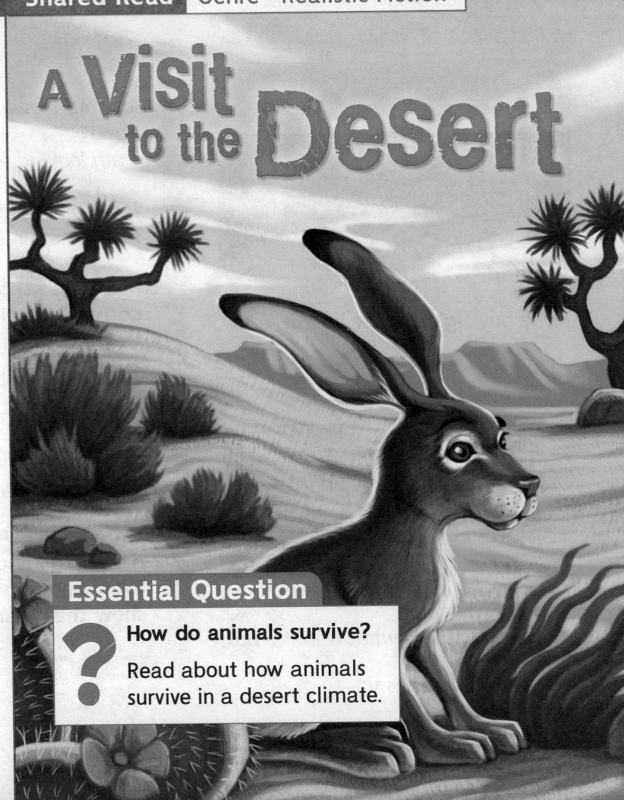

A Visit to the Desert

Essential Question

How do animals survive?

Read about how animals survive in a desert climate.

88

Tim was looking forward to this **vacation**. Then his parents told him the family would be visiting Grandma in Nevada. Tim was unhappy. He wanted to be with his friends this summer.

"Grandma is eager to see you," Mom said. "She can't wait to take you on a desert **hike**."

Text Evidence 🔍

① Specific Vocabulary Ⓐ🅒🆃

Find the word *vacation*. School is closed during a vacation. In the first sentence, circle how Tim feels about his vacation.

② Comprehension
Plot

Reread the first paragraph. Underline what Tim's parents tell him. Why does this make Tim feel unhappy? Box the sentence that tells you.

③ Sentence Structure Ⓐ🅒🆃

Reread the last paragraph. Circle the person the pronoun *she* refers to. Underline why this person is eager to see Tim.

Text Evidence

① Sentence Structure (A)(C)(T)

Box the comma in the third sentence. Circle the part of the sentence that tells what Grandma does as the family hikes.

COLLABORATE

② Talk About It

Discuss what Tim learns. What can the animals do in hot desert weather?

Animals find ways _____

_____

_____.

③ Specific Vocabulary (A)(C)(T)

The words *used to* can mean "comfortable with." Tim wonders if he can get used to something. Circle what that is.

The next morning Grandma met them at the airport. Then they drove to the desert. As they hiked, Grandma **explained** that animals enjoy the open desert space. It gives them the freedom to move from place to place. Tim learned that the animals find ways to adapt to the hot desert weather. He **wondered** if he could get **used to** the desert climate.

"Wow," Tim said, "look at that! The turtle carries its home on its back!"

Grandma smiled at Tim's excitement. "Actually," she said, "that is a desert tortoise. It looks for the shade made by the shadows of rocks. That's how it cools off. He burrows underground to get away from the heat." The tortoise **disappeared** into its burrow. Tim leaned over the hole. He could not hear a sound.

"I'll bet it likes the silence of its burrow," Tim **whispered**.

"I think it likes its sense of safety too," Grandma added.

1 Comprehension (A)(C)(T)
Plot

Reread the third sentence. Circle the word that tells about Tim's feelings in the middle of the story.

2 Specific Vocabulary (A)(C)(T)

The word *whispered* means "spoke in a very quiet way." Why does Tim whisper?

Tim thinks the tortoise likes

_____

_____

_____.

COLLABORATE

3 Talk About It

Discuss how a tortoise survives in the desert. Box two ways it stays cool. Where does it go for safety?

① Comprehension

Plot

Reread the second paragraph. Underline what Tim says about desert animals. What does he forget about after seeing these animals?

Tim forgets about _____

_____

COLLABORATE

② Talk About It

Talk about how a Great Horned Owl stays cool. Why does it hunt at night?

"That's the same feeling I get at home," Tim **sighed**. Just then a large rabbit hopped by. Grandma explained that the jack rabbit's large ears help it stay cool.

"These animals are so unlike the animals at home!" Tim said. He had forgotten about the desert heat.

"Some animals stay cool by sleeping during the day. Then they **hunt** at night," said Grandma. A Great Horned Owl hooted above them. Grandma said, "It will soon be time for the owl to hunt."

"Which means it's time for us to head back," Dad added.

"Aw, this vacation is **going by too fast**," Tim said. They asked Tim about the heat. "What heat?" Tim asked. "I feel as fresh and cool as a new flower. I've adapted!" Everyone laughed.

Greg Newbold

Make Connections

? How does the desert tortoise survive in the heat? ESSENTIAL QUESTION

Think of another animal you know. How does it survive in its climate? TEXT TO SELF

Text Evidence

1 **Specific Vocabulary** ACT

People say something is *going by too fast* when they do not want a fun time to end. Circle what Tim says is going by too fast.

2 **Comprehension**
Plot

Underline how Tim says he feels in the desert heat at the end of the story.

COLLABORATE

3 **Talk About It**

Talk about why everyone laughs at the end of the story. What does Tim mean when he says he adapted?

_____

_____

_____.

93

Partner Discussion Answer the questions. Discuss what you learned about "A Visit to the Desert." Write the page numbers where you found text evidence.

Why does the family visit the desert?

I read Grandma can't wait to _____.

As they hiked, Grandma _____.

Tim learned _____.

Text Evidence 🔍

Page(s): _____

Page(s): _____

Page(s): _____

What desert animals have learned to adapt?

The _____ burrows underground to _____.

I read that a _____ has large ears that _____.

Some animals sleep _____ and hunt _____.

Text Evidence 🔍

Page(s): _____

Page(s): _____

Page(s): _____

Group Discussion Present your answers to the group. Cite text evidence to justify your thinking. Listen to and discuss the group's opinions about your answers.

COLLABORATE

Write Review your notes. Then write your answer to the Essential Question. Use text evidence to support your answer. Use vocabulary words in your writing.

How do the animals survive in a desert climate?

The animals find ways to _____.

The desert tortoise _____

_____.

A jack rabbit _____

_____.

The Great Horned Owl _____

_____.

COLLABORATE

Share Writing Present your writing to the class. Discuss their opinions. Think about what the class says. Do they justify their claims? Explain why you agree or disagree with claims.

I agree with _____ because _____.

I disagree because _____.

Write to Sources

Olivia

pages 88–93

Take Notes About the Text I took notes about the text on the chart to respond to the prompt: *Add to the story. Tell about Grandma and Tim sitting outside at night.*

Grandma takes Tim on a desert hike.

↓

Desert animals adapt to the heat.

↓

The Great Horned Owl hunts at night to stay cool.

↓

Tim forgets about the desert heat.

Write About the Text I used my notes to add an event to the story.

Student Model: *Narrative Text*

Grandma and Tim sat outside together. Grandma said that the desert is as beautiful at night as it is in the day. It was cool outside in the dark. Tim saw something fly by. It was a Great Horned Owl!

Tim said, "The owl woke up because it is cool outside at night. The desert is busy at night!"

TALK ABOUT IT

COLLABORATE

Text Evidence Underline the desert animal Tim sees at night. Why did Olivia put this detail in her story?

Grammar Circle the three nouns in the second sentence. What does Grandma compare?

Connect Ideas Box the connecting word *because* in the sentence about the owl. Why does the owl wake up?

Your Turn

COLLABORATE

Add to the story. It is the end of Tim's vacation. Have Tim tell his Grandma how he feels about the desert.

>> *Go Digital*
Write your response online. Use your editing checklist.

TALK ABOUT IT

Weekly Concept Animals in Stories

? **Essential Question**
What can animals in stories teach us?

» *Go Digital*

FINISH

98

Describe what the animal characters are doing. What lesson do we learn from them? Write on the chart different lessons animals in stories teach us.

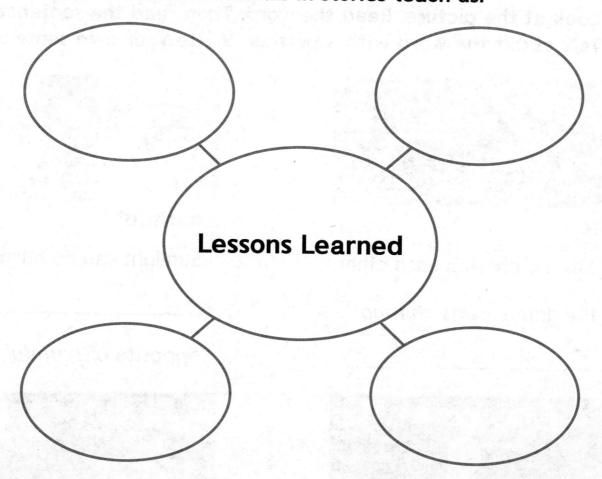

Lessons Learned

Discuss lessons that we learn from animal characters, such as the Tortoise and the Hare. Use the words from the chart. You can say:

We learn from Tortoise that _____.

We learn from Hare that _____.

More Vocabulary

Look at the picture. Read the word. Then read the sentence. Talk about the word with a partner. Write your own sentence.

chasing

The rabbits are **chasing** each other.

During the game, I was *chasing*

_____.

grab

Tom **grabs** the red pepper.

Tom *grabs* it because his family

_____.

harmful

Sunlight can be **harmful** to skin.

_____ means the

opposite of *harmful*.

real

Plastic flowers are not **real** flowers.

A _____

is not a *real* _____.

100

tricking

Some bugs hide by **tricking** animals.

I read a story about _____

tricking _____.

truth

Mom asks Joel to tell the **truth**.

To tell the *truth* means _____

_____.

Words and Phrases
Suffix *-ly*

A word with suffix *-ly* tells the way people or things do something.

quickly = in a quick way
Ted quickly ran to the park.

slowly = in a slow way
Liz walked slowly to school.

Read each sentence. Write a word with suffix *–ly* that means the same as the underlined words.

A rabbit ran _____ across the grass.

in a quick way

A turtle walked _____ to the pond.

in a slow way

>> Go Digital Add the words *quickly* and *slowly* to your New Words notebook. Write a sentence to show the meaning of each word.

COLLABORATE

❶ Talk About It

Look at the picture. Read the title. Talk about what you see. Write your ideas.

What does this title tell you?

_____

_____

_____.

What is the boy doing?

_____

_____.

Take notes as you read the text.

The Boy Who Cried Wolf

Essential Question

? **What can animals in stories teach us?**

Read to find out what a shepherd boy learns.

Long ago a **shepherd** boy sat on a hilltop watching the village sheep. He was not fond of his job. He didn't like it one bit. He would have liked something wonderful to happen, but nothing remarkable ever did.

The shepherd boy watched the clouds move softly by to stay busy. He saw horses, dogs, and dragons in the sky. He made up stories with these things as characters.

Peter Francis

❶ **Specific Vocabulary** Ⓐ Ⓒ Ⓣ

Find the word *shepherd*. A shepherd takes care of sheep. Underline where the shepherd boy watches the village sheep.

❷ **Comprehension**
Problem and Solution

Reread the first paragraph. Underline how the boy feels about his job. What is the problem?

The boy wants something

_____

_____ at his job.

❸ **Sentence Structure** Ⓐ Ⓒ Ⓣ

Reread the second paragraph. Circle the commas. Box the three things the boy sees in the sky.

103

1 Comprehension
Problem and Solution

Nothing remarkable happens at the boy's job. Underline what the boy does to solve this problem in the first paragraph.

2 Sentence Structure A C T

In the last paragraph, a comma separates two parts of the second sentence. Circle the part that tells what happens when the villagers get to top of the hill.

COLLABORATE

3 Talk About It

Talk about why the boy laughs. Underline what the villagers tell the boy after he laughs.

Then one day he had a better idea! He took a deep breath and cried out, "Wolf! Wolf! The wolf is **chasing** the sheep!"

The villagers ran up the hill to help the boy. When they got there, they saw no **harmful** wolf. The boy laughed. "Shepherd boy! Don't cry 'wolf!' unless there really is a wolf!" said the villagers. They went back down the hill.

That afternoon the boy again cried out, "Wolf! Wolf! The wolf is chasing the sheep!"

The villagers ran to help the boy again. They saw no wolf. The villagers were angry. "Don't cry 'wolf!' when there is NO WOLF!" they said. The shepherd boy just smiled. The villagers went quickly down the hill again.

Peter Francis

❶ Specific Vocabulary Ⓐ Ⓒ Ⓣ

The words *that afternoon* mean "the afternoon of the same day." Underline what the boy cries that afternoon.

❷ Comprehension

Reread the second paragraph. What do the villagers do again?

_____

_____

_____.

COLLABORATE

❸ Talk About It

Discuss why the villagers are angry.

Text Evidence

1 **Comprehension**
Problem and Solution

What problem does the boy have later that afternoon?

The boy sees _____

_____

2 **Sentence Structure** Ⓐ Ⓒ Ⓣ

Reread the last sentence in the first paragraph. The word *so* connects two ideas. Circle why the villagers do not come to help the boy.

3 **Specific Vocabulary** Ⓐ Ⓒ Ⓣ

Find the word *weeping*. Circle the context clue to the meaning of *weeping*. Why is the boy weeping?

The flock _____

_____

That afternoon the boy saw a **REAL** wolf. He did not want the wolf to **grab** any of the sheep! The boy thought the wolf would snatch one of them for a delicious, tasty meal. A sheep would be a big feast for a wolf. He quickly jumped to his feet and cried, "WOLF! WOLF!" The villagers thought he was **tricking** them again, so they did not come.

That night the shepherd boy did not return with their sheep. The villagers found the boy **weeping** real tears. "There really was a wolf here!" he said. "The flock ran away! When I cried out, 'Wolf! Wolf!' no one came. Why didn't you come?"

A kind man talked to the boy as they walked slowly back to the village. "In the morning, we'll help you look for the sheep," he said. "You have just learned one of life's important lessons. This is something you need to know. Nobody believes a person who tells lies. It is always better to tell the **truth!**"

Peter Francis

Make Connections

What did you learn after reading this animal story? ESSENTIAL QUESTION

Tell how you are similar or different from the shepherd boy. TEXT TO SELF

Text Evidence

❶ **Comprehension**
Problem and Solution

Reread the page. Circle who talks to the boy. Underline the words that tell how the villagers will help the boy.

COLLABORATE

❷ **Talk About It**

Discuss what the boy learns about telling lies. What is the lesson the boy learns?

_____

_____

_____

_____.

Respond to the Text

Partner Discussion **Answer the questions. Discuss what you learned about "The Boy Who Cried Wolf." Write the page numbers where you found text evidence.**

Why does the boy get the idea to cry wolf?

The boy doesn't like his job because _____.

When he cries wolf, _____.

The villagers are angry because _____.

| Text Evidence 🔍 |
| Page(s): _____ |
| Page(s): _____ |
| Page(s): _____ |

What does the boy do when a real wolf comes?

I read that the boy _____ but _____.

That night the boy does not return because _____.

A kind man helps the boy learn that _____.

| Text Evidence 🔍 |
| Page(s): _____ |
| Page(s): _____ |
| Page(s): _____ |

COLLABORATE **Group Discussion** **Present your answers to the group. Cite text evidence for your ideas. Listen to and discuss the group's opinions about your answers.**

Write Review your notes. Then write your answer to the Essential Question. Use text evidence to support your answer. Use vocabulary words in your writing.

What lesson can we learn from this animal story?

A shepherd boy does not like his job so he _____

_____.

When a real wolf comes _____

_____.

In the end, we learn that _____

_____.

Share Writing Present your writing to the class. Discuss their opinions. Think about what the class has to say. Do they justify their claims? Explain why you agree or disagree with their claims.

I agree with _____ because _____.

I disagree because _____.

Write to Sources

pages 102–107

Mia

Take Notes About the Text I took notes on this web to respond to the prompt: *Add to the story. Have the boy tell the villagers he is sorry.*

The boy cries, "Wolf!" The villagers run to help.

Nobody runs to help when a real wolf comes.

The villagers help the boy find the sheep.

Nobody believes a person who tells lies.

Write About the Text **I used my notes to add narrative text to the story.**

Student Model: *Narrative Text*

The shepherd boy sat with the villagers. He said, "I am sorry that I lied. I learned something important. I learned a lesson. I will not lie again."

In the morning, the villagers helped the boy find the sheep. After that, he always told the truth.

COLLABORATE

TALK ABOUT IT

Text Evidence **Underline** how the villagers help the boy. What do they help him do?

Grammar **Circle** the noun in the first sentence that names more than one. How do you know it is a plural noun?

Condense Ideas **Box** the two sentences that tell what the boy learns. How can you condense the ideas to make one sentence?

COLLABORATE

Your Turn

It is the next day. Tell how the boy takes care of the sheep.

>> *Go Digital*
Write your response online. Use your editing checklist.

TALK ABOUT IT

? **Essential Question**
What are features of different animal habitats?

» *Go Digital*

COLLABORATE

Describe the habitat of the owl in the picture. Write on the chart the features of a forest habitat.

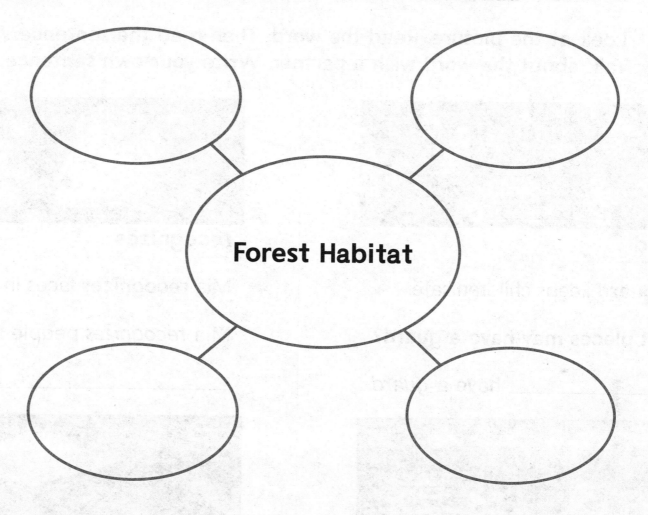

Forest Habitat

Discuss the different features of the owl's habitat. Use the words from the chart. You can say:

Some features of a forest habitat are _____

where animals _____.

More Vocabulary

COLLABORATE

Look at the picture. Read the word. Then read the sentence. Talk about the word with a partner. Write your own sentence.

guard

The **guard** keeps children safe.

What places may have a guard?

_____ have a *guard*.

hide

Squirrels **hide** nuts for winter.

Squirrels *hide* food _____

_____.

recognizes

Mia **recognizes** faces in the picture.

Mia *recognizes* people she

_____.

slip

I **slip** the mail into the slot.

To *slip* can mean to _____

_____.

warning

The lion gives a **warning** to stay away.

An animal gives a *warning* when

_____.

watchful

The mother is **watchful** of her baby.

A mother is *watchful* because she

_____.

Words and Phrases
Suffix *-er*

A word with suffix *-er* can be used to compare things.

high   *higher*

My kite flew <u>high</u>, but your kite flew <u>higher</u>.

cool   *cooler*

Yesterday was <u>cool</u>, but today is even <u>cooler</u>.

Read the sentences below. Circle the correct word for each blank.

An eagle builds a nest _____ than a bluebird.

high   *higher*

Our classroom is _____ than the library.

cool   *cooler*

>> Go Digital Add the words *higher* and *cooler* to your New Words notebook. Write a sentence to show the meaning of each.

COLLABORATE

① Talk About It

Look at the photos. Read the title. Talk about what you see. Write your ideas.

What does the title tell you?

_____

_____

_____.

What is the animal doing?

_____

_____

_____.

Take notes as you read the text.

A Prairie Guard Dog

Essential Question

? What are features of different animal habitats?

Read to learn about the place a prairie dog calls home.

Jeff Foott/Getty Images

I am on a journey. My trip is to a prairie. It is in the outdoor world called nature. Many animals live in a prairie habitat. This place has what prairie dogs need to survive. A prairie has a lot of grasses but few trees. Without places to **hide**, a prairie can be dangerous for some animals.

Good Morning!

It is early in the morning. First, I see a prairie dog. I name him Pete. He peeks his head out of his burrow underground. He looks around. Then Pete calls loudly to his family, "Yip!" He **lets them know** it is safe to come out. Soon four prairie dogs come out.

Prairie dogs build underground burrows to be safe from predators.

Text Evidence

1 Comprehension

Main Topic and Key Details

Reread the first paragraph. Circle the name of the habitat where prairie dogs live. What plants grow in this habitat?

_____

_____

2 Specific Vocabulary (A)(C)(T)

Reread the second paragraph. The phrase *lets them know* means "tells." How does Pete let his family know it is safe to come out?

_____

_____

117

Text Evidence

1 Sentence Structure ACT

Reread the first sentence. Circle the word *and*. Underline the two ideas that the word *and* connects.

2 Comprehension
Main Topic and Key Details

Reread the second sentence. Underline why Pete cannot rest when he is the guard.

COLLABORATE

3 Talk About It

Talk about what Pete's work allows his family to do. Write two of the activities.

_____

_____

_____.

118

Pete is the **guard** and he is restless. He cannot rest because he is always looking around for danger. This allows the other prairie dogs to safely munch on grasses and seeds. They can also groom each other or work on their burrow.

Yap!
Yap!

Prairie dogs can make 11 different sounds to communicate with each other.

(bkgd) Bob Stefko/Getty Images; Jeff Foott/Getty Images

A Scare

Oh no! Pete spies a large badger! When he sees it, he gives a loud bark, "Yap! Yap!" His family **recognizes** the **warning**. Some hide in tall grasses, and some jump into the burrow. The badger runs at Pete, but the **watchful** guard is able to escape into the burrow. I am glad he is able to **get away** from danger.

After a few minutes, Pete peeks his head out again and he is back on the job.

Badgers live on prairies and hunt prairie dogs.

Text Evidence

① Sentence Structure Ⓐ Ⓒ Ⓣ

Reread the second and third sentences. Circle the noun the pronoun *it* refers to. When does Pete give a loud bark?

Pete gives a loud bark when

_____

a _____.

COLLABORATE

② Talk About It

Talk about what happens after Pete gives the warning. Underline the ways Pete's family stays safe.

③ Specific Vocabulary Ⓐ Ⓒ Ⓣ

Find the phrase *get away*. Circle the word in the paragraph with almost the same meaning. Box where Pete gets away from danger.

119

Text Evidence

1 Sentence Structure (A)(C)(T)

A comma separates two parts in the first sentence. Underline the sentence part that tells why it is hot now.

2 Specific Vocabulary (A)(C)(T)

Reread the fourth sentence. Circle the clue to the meaning of *tunnels*. Box where the tunnels lead to.

3 Comprehension

Main Topic and Key Details

Reread the rest of the page. Underline details that tell how each room is used. What foods do the prairie dogs keep in the burrow to eat later?

They eat buried _____

and _____.

Break Time

The sun gets higher, and it is hot now. The prairie dogs **slip** into their deep burrow where it is cooler. Even Pete goes in. **Tunnels**, like hallways, lead to different areas. There is a sleeping room. There is a room used like a bathroom. The prairie dogs cover up roots and seeds in one room. Later, they eat the buried food there.

DEA Picture Library/Getty Images

Second Shift

I keep watching the burrow. Finally, the sun begins to set and a different prairie dog peeks its head out. I name him Gary. Pete must be **off duty**. "Yip," Gary calls. The other prairie dogs come back out.

The prairie dogs eat and play until the moon is high in the sky. Then they go to sleep in their burrows. I wonder if Pete will be back on duty. I will see in the morning.

Prairie Dog Facts

Size	12 to 15 inches tall
Weight	2 to 4 pounds
Habitat	short and medium grass desert prairies
Food	roots, seeds, leaves of plants, grasses
Shelter	underground burrows with many rooms
Predators	coyotes, bobcats, badgers, foxes, weasels

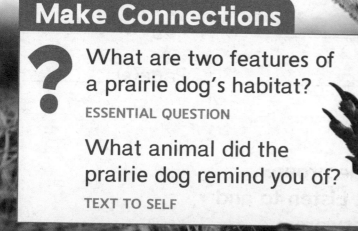

Make Connections

?

What are two features of a prairie dog's habitat?

ESSENTIAL QUESTION

What animal did the prairie dog remind you of?

TEXT TO SELF

Text Evidence 🔍

❶ Comprehension

Main Topic and Key Details

Read the first paragraph. Underline details that support the idea that Gary is a guard like Pete.

❷ Specific Vocabulary Ⓐ Ⓒ Ⓣ

Pete must be *off duty* because he is not working. Reread the second paragraph. Circle the phrase that means the opposite of *off duty*. Box when Pete may be back working.

COLLABORATE

❸ Talk About It

Discuss facts in the chart. How do prairie dogs use grasses in their habitat?

_____

_____

(bkgd) Bob Stefko/Getty Images

121

Respond to the Text

Partner Discussion Answer the questions. Discuss what you learned about "A Prairie Guard Dog." Write the page numbers where you found text evidence.

COLLABORATE

What is Pete's job as a guard?

In the morning, Pete _____.

Pete looks around _____.

When a badger appears, Pete _____.

Text Evidence 🔍

Page(s): _____

Page(s): _____

Page(s): _____

Why is a prairie dog's burrow important?

When there is danger, _____.

When the sun is high in the sky, _____.

The burrow has areas for _____.

Text Evidence 🔍

Page(s): _____

Page(s): _____

Page(s): _____

Group Discussion Present your answers to the group. Cite text evidence to justify your thinking. Listen to and discuss the group's opinions about your answers.

COLLABORATE

Write Review your notes. Then write your answer to the Essential Question. Use text evidence to support your answer. Use vocabulary words in your writing.

What are some important features of a prairie dog's habitat?

A prairie has _____.

Prairie dogs eat _____.

Prairie dogs live in a _____.

The home has _____

_____.

Share Writing Present your writing to the class. Discuss their opinions. Think about what the class has to say. Do they justify their claims? Explain why you agree or disagree with their claims.

I agree with _____ because _____.

I disagree because _____.

Write to Sources

Stella

Take Notes About the Text I took notes to answer the question: *How does the author organize the text about a prairie dog's day?*

pages 116–121

"It is early in the morning."

↓

"The sun gets higher, and it is hot now."

↓

"The prairie dogs eat and play
until the moon is high in the sky."

Write About the Text **I wrote about how the author organized the text.**

The author describes a prairie dog's day from morning to night. First, the author says that it is early in the morning. Then the author shows it is the middle of the day with the detail "the sun gets higher." Finally, the author writes about the moon high in the sky. This shows that it is night. The author ends the text now because it is the end of the day.

TALK ABOUT IT

COLLABORATE

Text Evidence **Underline** the detail that tells what happens after morning. What time of day does it describe?

Grammar In the first sentence, **circle** a phrase that tells about a day. How are the events in the text organized?

Connect Ideas **Box** the connecting word in the last sentence. Why does the text end at this time?

Your Turn

COLLABORATE

Answer the questions: What does the chart on page 121 tell you? How does it help you understand prairie dogs?

≫ Go Digital
Write your response online. Use your editing checklist.

Weekly Concept Baby Animals

? **Essential Question**
How are offspring like their parents?

>> *Go Digital*

COLLABORATE

What are ways the baby penguin, or offspring, is like its mother? How are the two birds different? Write ways offspring and their parents are the same and different on the chart.

Same	Different

Discuss ways baby animals are the same and different from their parents. Use the words from the chart. You can say:

The baby penguin and its mother are alike because

_____.

Some ways a baby penguin is different from its mother are

_____.

COLLABORATE Look at the picture. Read the word. Then read the sentence. Talk about the word with a partner. Write your own sentence.

hatch

Baby birds **hatch** from eggs.

I saw _____ *hatch* _____

_____.

helpless

Kittens are **helpless** babies.

A *helpless* kitten needs _____

_____.

powerful

A horse is a **powerful** animal.

The *powerful* horse can _____

_____.

safety

The turtle hides for **safety**.

What is the opposite of safety?

_____

soar

The birds **soar** through the sky.

I saw _____

soar _____ .

tops

The nests are in the **tops** of trees.

A squirrel _____

_____ the *tops* of trees.

Words and Phrases
Conjunctions *until* and *when*

The words *until* and *when* connect two ideas in a sentence.

Until **and *when* tell about time.**

I cannot go outside <u>until</u> the rain stops.

We will eat lunch <u>when</u> Dad gets home.

Read the sentences below. Write the correct conjunction to complete each sentence.

A puppy cannot learn tricks _____ it is older.

until   when

My family will take a trip _____ school is out.

until   when

>> Go Digital Add the words *until* and *when* to your New Words notebook. Write a sentence to show the meaning of each.

(t)Scott Flaherty/USFWS; (b)fotolinchen/iStock/360/Getty Images

COLLABORATE

1 Talk About It

Look at the photo. Read the title. Talk about what you see. Write your ideas.

What does the title tell you?

_____

_____

_____.

What is the adult eagle doing?

_____

_____

_____

Take notes as you read the text.

Eagles and Eaglets

Essential Question

?

How are offspring like their parents?

Read to learn how young bald eagles are like their parents.

Bald eagles are birds. The baby birds, or offspring are called eaglets. Let's read about how eaglets are like their parents.

It's Nesting Time

All birds **lay eggs**. Bald eagles build their nests in the **tops** of trees so the eggs will be safe. Their nests are built of sticks and grass. They add on to their nests each year. They can become huge! These giant nests can be as large as nine feet across. That's bigger than your bed!

The mother eagle lays from one to three eggs. She sits on her eggs until they **hatch**. Then both parents watch over the nest.

❶ Comprehension
Main Topic and Key Details

In the first paragraph, the author tells what the text is about. Box the sentence that tells the main topic of "Eagles and Eaglets."

❷ Specific Vocabulary Ⓐ Ⓒ Ⓣ

A bald eagle *lays eggs*, or makes eggs, in her nest. Underline what bald eagles do so the eggs will be safe.

❸ Sentence Structure Ⓐ Ⓒ Ⓣ

Reread the last two sentences. Circle the word that connects the two sentences. Underline what happens when an eagle's eggs hatch.

① Comprehension
Main Topic and Key Details

Reread the first paragraph. Underline key details that explain why eaglets are helpless.

② Sentence Structure Ⓐ Ⓒ Ⓣ

Look back to the fifth and sixth sentences. Underline the noun that the pronoun *they* refers to. Box the text that tells why "they do not have milk to feed their young."

COLLABORATE

③ Talk About It

Talk about what eagles use to hunt. Why must eaglets learn to use these things?

Proud Parents

At first the eaglets are **helpless**. They cannot walk. They need their parents for food. They also cannot see well. Birds are not mammals. They do not have milk to feed their young. They hunt for food. Eaglets also need their parents for **safety**.

Eaglets Grow Up

Bald eagles use their sharp eyes to hunt. They use their strong wings to fly fast. They also use their claws and beak to catch fish. Young eaglets must learn all these things. Then they can live on their own.

The eagles must bring food to the eaglets.

Unlike mammals, birds have feathers, not fur. An eaglet is born covered with soft gray **down**. It cannot fly until it grows dark feathers like its parents. The eaglet stays near the nest until its wings grow strong. That takes about five months.

Bald Eagle

powerful eyes

dark feathers on body and wings

hooked yellow beak

white tail feathers

long claws

Frank Leung/Getty Images

❶ **Specific Vocabulary** Ⓐ Ⓒ Ⓣ

The word *down* means "small, soft feathers" in the text. Underline the sentence that tells why an eaglet cannot fly.

❷ **Comprehension**
Main Topic and Key Details

Reread the last two sentences. Circle the time it takes for an eaglet's wings to grow strong.

COLLABORATE

❸ **Talk About It**

Talk about the picture. How are the feathers of adults and eaglets different?

An eaglet has gray down.

_____

_____.

133

1 Comprehension

Main Topic and Key Details

Reread the page. Underline the detail that explains when an eaglet becomes an adult. Circle how long this takes.

2 Specific Vocabulary ACT

The phrase *up to* is used to tell how long something can happen. Box how long an eagle can stay alive.

COLLABORATE

3 Talk About It

Talk about the caption and the picture. What happens to an eagle's feathers when it soars?

_____

_____.

An eaglet becomes an adult when it has learned to do all the things its parents do. This takes about five years. Bald eagles can stay alive for **up to** thirty years.

When the bald eagle soars, the feathers on its huge wings spread out like fingers.

Bald Eagles Soar

Once it learns to fly, the bald eagle can **soar** for hours. The bald eagle must take good care of its feathers. It uses its beak to groom itself. It must keep its feathers clean. Can you believe this **powerful** eagle began life as a helpless baby?

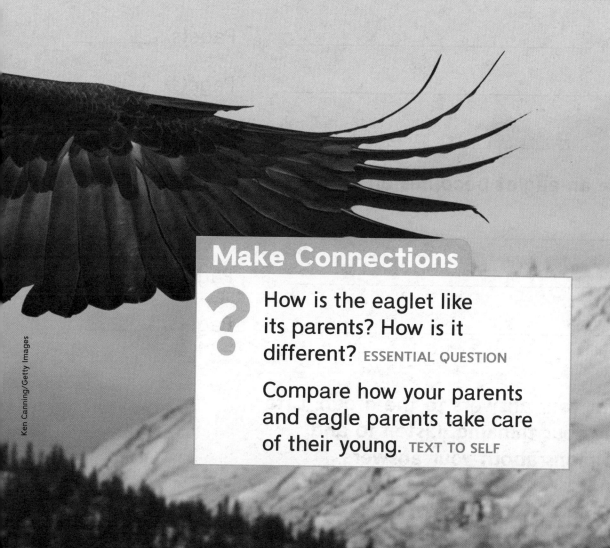

Ken Canning/Getty Images

Make Connections

How is the eaglet like its parents? How is it different? ESSENTIAL QUESTION

Compare how your parents and eagle parents take care of their young. TEXT TO SELF

Text Evidence

1 Sentence Structure ⒶⒸⓉ

A comma separates two parts of the first sentence. Underline the part that tells when a bald eagle can soar for hours.

2 Comprehension

Reread the paragraph. How does a bald eagle groom, or clean, its feathers?

_____

_____

_____

COLLABORATE

3 Talk About It

Discuss the question at the end of the text. Circle the adjectives that tell how eagles and eaglets are very different.

135

Respond to the Text

Partner Discussion Answer the questions. Discuss what you learned about "Eagles and Eaglets." Write the page numbers where you found text evidence.

How do eagle parents care for their young?

Eagles build nests _____.

After the eggs hatch, _____.

Eaglets cannot _____.

Text Evidence 🔍

Page(s): _____

Page(s): _____

Page(s): _____

What happens once an eaglet becomes an adult?

An eaglet grows _____.

In about five years, _____.

The eaglet now _____.

Text Evidence 🔍

Page(s): _____

Page(s): _____

Page(s): _____

Group Discussion Present your answers to the group. Cite text evidence to justify your thinking. Listen to and discuss the group's opinions about your answers.

Write Review your notes. Then write your answer to the Essential Question. Use text evidence to support your answer. Use vocabulary words in your writing.

How are the offspring of bald eagles like their parents?

All bald eagles are _____.

At first eaglets are _____.

Eaglets have feathers called _____.

Later they will _____.

They can now _____

_____.

Share Writing Present your writing to the class. Discuss their opinions. Think about what the class has to say. Do they justify their claims? Explain why you agree or disagree with their claims.

I agree with _____ because _____.

I disagree because _____.

Write to Sources

Nick

pages 130–135

Take Notes About the Text I took notes on this chart to answer the question: *Do you think eaglets are more like or different from their parents?*

Eaglets	Parents
helpless	take care of eaglets in nests
get food from their parents	hunt for food
soft, gray down	dark feathers

Write About the Text I used my notes to write an opinion about eagles and eaglets.

Student Model: *Opinion*

I think eaglets are different from their parents. They are helpless. They get food from their parents. Their parents can hunt for food. Eaglets have soft, gray down. Their parents have dark feathers. Eaglets and their parents are very different.

TALK ABOUT IT

Text Evidence **Circle** details that tell how the birds get food. Why does Nick include these details in his paragraph?

Grammar **Box** the plural nouns in the first sentence. Why are they plural?

Connect Ideas **Underline** the sentences that tell how eaglets and eagles look. How can you combine the sentences to connect the ideas?

Your Turn

Do you think it is easy or hard for a parent to take care of an eaglet? Use details from the text in your answer.

>> Go Digital
Write your response online. Use your editing checklist.

139

TALK ABOUT IT

Weekly Concept Animals in Poems

? Essential Question
What do we love about animals?

>> *Go Digital*

140

COLLABORATE

How does the boy feel about swimming with the dolphin? Talk about a dolphin or another animal. Then write words that tell all about the animal on the chart.

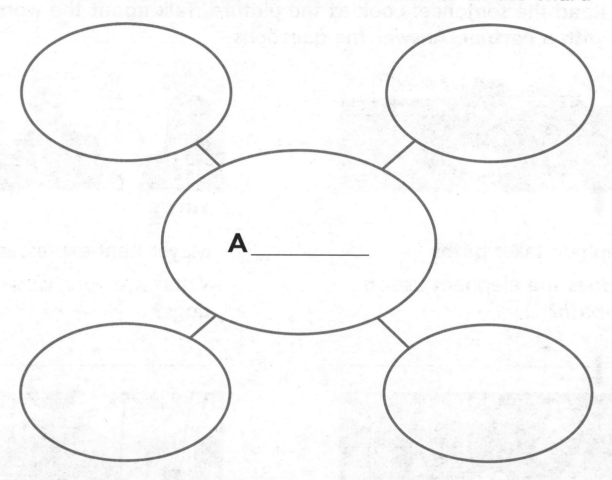

A_____

Discuss words that can be used to describe your animal. Use the words from the chart. You can say:

A _____ looks _____.

It feels _____.

It does _____.

More Vocabulary

Read the sentence. Look at the picture. Talk about the word with a partner. Answer the questions.

baths

The elephant takes **baths**.

What does the elephant use to take a *bath***?**

_____

views

Mayor Kent expresses his **views**.

What are your *views* **about dogs?**

_____

pounce

Puppies **pounce** during play.

What word means almost the same as *pounce***?**

_____

sway

We saw the trees **sway**.

What makes a tree *sway***?**

_____

Poetry Terms

poem

Authors can express their feelings or imagination in a **poem**.

Read a short poem about watching a bird.

High above a bird flew.
I would like to be a bird, too!

rhyme

The words **fox** and **box** **rhyme**.

They end in the same sound.

word choice

The snow is sparkling.

The word *sparkling* is a good **word choice** to describe snow.

COLLABORATE

Use these words to write a poem with a partner.

bee me tree

I see a _____.

flying to a _____.

Does this bee

see _____?

Circle the more descriptive word in each sentence.

The playful kitten *pounces/jumps* on a toy.

Trees *sway/move* in the wind.

143

1 **Literary Elements**

Word Choice

Reread lines one and two in the poem. Write how cats and kittens express their views.

_____

_____

COLLABORATE

2 **Talk About It**

Talk about the orange cat in the picture. Reread lines three and four. Box what a cat uses to stay clean.

3 **Literary Elements**

Rhyme

Reread lines five and six. Circle the words that rhyme. Underline what the author wonders, or tries to imagine.

Cats and Kittens

Essential Question

? **What do we love about animals?**

Read how poets describe animals they love.

(l) Martin Poole/Digital Vision/Getty Images; (mouse) D. Hurst/Alamy

Cats and kittens express their **views**
With hisses, purrs, and little mews.

Instead of taking **baths** like me,
They use their tongues quite handily.

I wonder what my mom would say
If I tried cleaning up that way.

They stay as still as still can be,
Until a mouse they chance to see.

And then in one great **flash** of fur
They **pounce** on a toy with a PURRRR.

— by Constance Keremes

1 Comprehension
Key Details

Look back at the seventh and eighth lines. Circle what a cat or kitten does until it sees a mouse.

2 Specific Vocabulary

Reread the last two lines. The word *flash* tells about something that moves quickly. Write the words that describe how a cat pounces on a toy.

_____

_____

❶ Comprehension
Key Details

Reread lines three and four of the poem. There are three details about camels. Circle each detail.

❷ Specific Vocabulary ⒶⒸⓉ

Read lines five and six. The word *bouncy* means "moves up and down." Underline other words the author uses to describe a ride on a camel.

❸ Literary Elements
Poem

Underline two lines in the poem that tell you the author likes camels.

Desert Camels

Camels have a hump on their backs
To carry people and their sacks.

They're very strong, don't mind the Sun,
Won't stop for drinks until they're done.

They give people a **bouncy** ride.
They **sway** and move from side to side.

I'd like a camel for a pet,
But haven't asked my mother yet!

— by Martine Wren

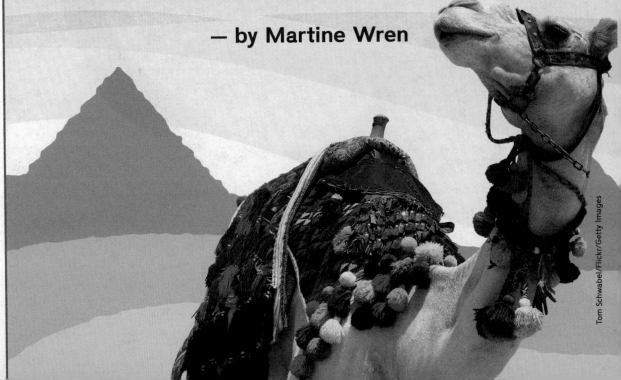

Tom Schwabel/Flickr/Getty Images

A Bat Is Not a Bird

A bat has neither feathers nor beak.
He does not chirp, just gives a shriek.

He flies by hearing sounds like pings,
Flapping, flapping his leathery wings.

At night when I'm asleep in my bed,
He gets to fly around instead!

— by Trevor Reynolds

Make Connections

? Talk about what the poet loves about the animal in each poem. ESSENTIAL QUESTION

Describe how your favorite animal behaves. TEXT TO SELF

T. Walker/Photri Images/Alamy

Text Evidence

❶ Comprehension
Key Details

Reread lines one and two of the poem. Underline details that explain how a bat is not a bird.

A bird chirps. What sound does a bat make?

A bat _____

_____.

❷ Literary Elements
Word Choice

Reread lines three and four. Circle the word the author uses to describe a bat's wings.

COLLABORATE

❸ Talk About It

Reread the last two lines. Discuss what the author thinks about. Underline what bats get to do.

147

Respond to the Text

Partner Discussion Answer the questions. Discuss what you learned about "Cats and Kittens." Write where you found text evidence.

What does the author describe about cats and kittens?	**Text Evidence** 🔍
She tells how cats and kittens express _____.	Line(s): _____
They take baths _____.	Line(s): _____
The author wonders _____.	Line(s): _____
She describes how they stay _____.	Line(s): _____
They pounce _____.	Line(s): _____

Group Discussion Present your answers to the group. Cite text evidence to justify your thinking. Listen to and discuss the group's opinions about your answers.

Write Review your notes about "Cats and Kittens." Then write your answer to the Essential Question. Use text evidence to support your answer. Use vocabulary words in your writing.

What does the author love about cats and kittens?

The author shows how cats and kittens express _____

_____.

They use their _____.

Cats and kittens stay still until _____

_____.

Then they _____.

Share Writing Present your writing to the class. Discuss their opinions. Think about what the class has to say. Do they justify their claims? Explain why you agree or disagree with their claims.

I agree with _____ because _____.

I disagree with _____ because _____.

pages 144–147

Martin

Take Notes About the Text I took notes on the chart to answer the questions: *Which words do the authors use that rhyme? How do you know?*

Poem	Lines That Rhyme
"Cats and Kittens"	Cats and kittens express their views With hisses, purrs, and little mews.
"Desert Camels"	Camels have a hump on their backs To carry people and their sacks.
"Desert Camels"	They're very strong, don't mind the Sun, Won't stop for drinks until they're done.

Write About the Text I used my notes from my chart to answer the questions.

Student Model: *Informative Text*

The authors rhyme the last word in each line. Words that rhyme end in the same sound. In "Cats and Kittens," the author used the rhyming words "views" and "mews." In "Desert Camels," the author used the rhyming words "backs" and "sacks." The author used the rhyming words "Sun" and "done." All of the poems have words that rhyme.

COLLABORATE

TALK ABOUT IT

Text Evidence **Circle** the words from "Cats and Kittens" that come from the chart. How do you know the words rhyme?

Grammar **Box** the last sentence in Martin's paragraph. How can you add the word *many* in the sentence?

Condense Ideas **Underline** the sentences about "Desert Camels." How can you combine the sentences?

COLLABORATE

Your Turn

Explain how the author uses rhyming words and lines in "A Bat Is Not a Bird."

>> Go Digital
Write your response online. Use your editing checklist.

Live and Learn

The Big Idea

What have you learned about the world that surprises you?

Lane Oatey/Blue Jean Images/Getty Images; (inset) Eric Bean/Photodisc/Getty Images

TALK ABOUT IT

Weekly Concept The Earth's Forces

? **Essential Question**
How do the Earth's forces affect us?

>> *Go Digital*

154

COLLABORATE

Describe what the boy is doing. What force is pulling him down the slide? Write other examples of gravity at work on the web.

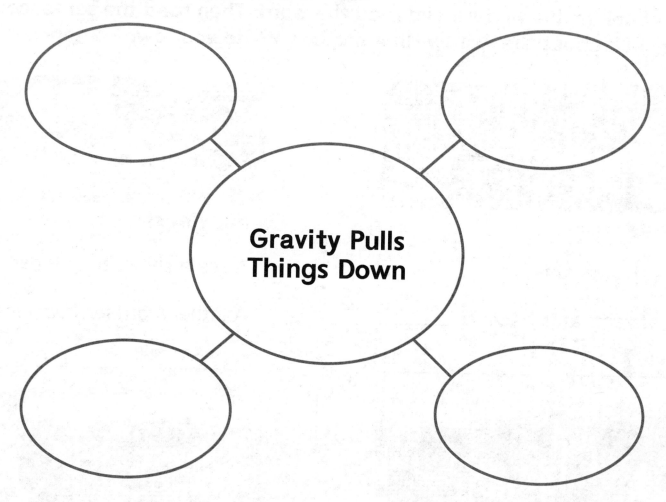

Gravity Pulls Things Down

Discuss examples of the force of gravity at work. Use the words from the chart. You can say:

The force of gravity pulls _____.

Gravity also pulls _____.

More Vocabulary

Look at the picture and read the word. Then read the sentence. Talk about the word with a partner. Write your own sentence.

attracts

Food **attracts** ants.

Food *attracts* ants because _____

_____.

appears

The kids **appear** to be curious.

_____ *appears* to be

_____.

heaviness

A scale shows **heaviness**.

Another word for *heaviness* is

_____.

tight

The lid on the jar is **tight**.

The lid is *tight* so _____

_____.

wish

The fans **wish** for a win today.

I *wish* _____

_____ .

wooden

Dad built a **wooden** fence.

A *wooden* fence is made of

_____ .

Words and Phrases

than, as . . . as

Phrases with *than* compare things that are not equal, or not the same.
Sam is <u>taller than</u> Ed.

Phrases with *as . . . as* help compare things that are equal, or the same.
Ed is <u>as tall as</u> Paul.

Read the sentences. Box the phrase that compares two things that are not equal. Circle the phrase that compares two things that are equal.

A car is faster than a bike.

The grapes are as sweet as the apples.

Write sentences using *than* and *as . . . as*.

_____

_____

>> Go Digital Add *than* and *as . . . as* to your New Words notebook. Include your sentences.

COLLABORATE

1 Talk About It

Look at the photograph. Read the title. Talk about what you see. Write your ideas.

What does this title tell you about the text?

_____

_____

_____.

What is the girl in the photograph doing?

_____

_____

_____.

Take notes as you read the text.

158

Magnets Work!

Essential Question

? How do the Earth's forces affect us?

Read to learn about magnets and how they help us.

©Mike Kemp/Rubberball/Corbis

Did you know magnets are all around you? Magnets help you do amazing things! Keep reading! See if you think magnets have surprising uses.

Magnets Pull

Look closely and you will see. Magnets can be found on a can opener. The magnet **attracts**, or pulls, the lid off of a soup can. A push or pull is called a force.

There is also a magnet in a refrigerator. It pulls the metal in the door to make a **tight seal**. Do you know how?

Martin Leigh/Oxford Scientific/Getty Images

Text Evidence

COLLABORATE

❶ Talk About It

Talk about objects that a magnet attracts. What does a magnet not attract?

It does not attract objects

made of _____

or _____.

❷ Comprehension
Author's Purpose

Reread the second paragraph. Underline what all magnets have.

Look back at the diagram. What does the author explain about unlike poles?

A north pole and south pole

_____

_____.

A magnet's force pulls objects made of metals called iron and steel. It will not pull other things. It will not pull a **wooden** pencil or a plastic toy. A magnet does not attract all items.

Magnets Have Poles

You have proved, or shown, that magnets can pull some things to it. Why is this true? The two ends of a magnet are its poles. Every magnet has a north pole and a south pole.

North Pole — South Pole

Unlike poles attract each other.

Steve Schell

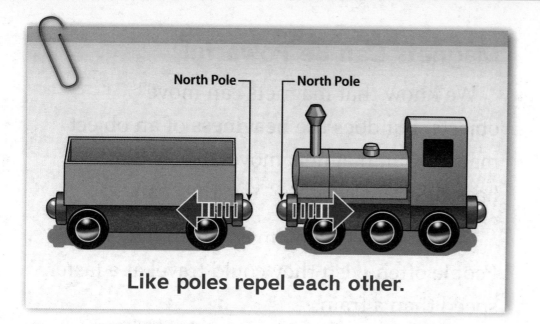

North Pole — North Pole

Like poles repel each other.

Have you ever played with trains that have magnets? Sometimes, you try to put two train cars together, but they **repel**. This means they push away from each other.

Then you turn one of the cars around. The two cars snap together as quick as a wink. That's right! If you have played with these trains, you know it is true.

When the train cars push away, two of the same poles are facing each other. However, if you put the north and south poles together, they will snap together like the train.

Steve Schell

Text Evidence 🔍

1 Comprehension

Author's Purpose

Reread the subheading and first paragraph. What can magnets do that is powerful?

Magnets can move objects

_____

_____.

2 Specific Vocabulary (A)(C)(T)

Find the word *scientists*. Some scientists study how magnets work. Circle what scientists are doing with magnets.

Magnets Can Be Powerful

We know that magnets can move objects. But does the **heaviness** of an object matter? Can magnets move objects that have different weights? Yes, they can.

Scientists are using magnets in new ways. People often **wish** they could travel at a faster speed than a train.

The magnets on this train make it float over the track.

Bernd Mellmann/Alamy

There is a new train that uses powerful magnets to travel more quickly. Magnets lift the train above the track and push the train forward. The train **appears** to be moving as fast as lightning! Scientists have measured these train speeds. They are much faster than the trains we know.

Can you imagine what magnets will help us do in the future?

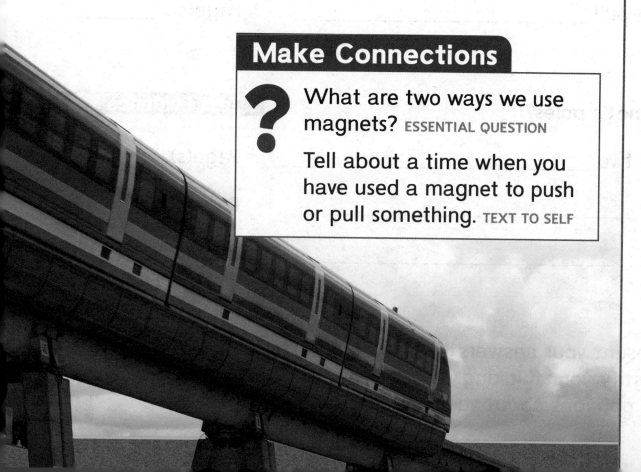

Make Connections

? What are two ways we use magnets? ESSENTIAL QUESTION

Tell about a time when you have used a magnet to push or pull something. TEXT TO SELF

Text Evidence

1 Sentence Structure Ⓐ Ⓒ Ⓣ

Reread the second sentence. The word *and* connects the actions that magnets do to move the train. Circle the two actions.

COLLABORATE

2 Talk About It

Will magnets make train travel faster? Underline details to support your ideas.

3 Comprehension
Author's Purpose

Reread the question in the last paragraph. What does the author want readers to think about?

_____

_____

_____

Respond to the Text

COLLABORATE

Partner Discussion Answer the questions. Discuss what you learned about "Magnets Work!" Write the page numbers where you found text evidence.

What can a magnet pull?	**Text Evidence**
Magnets can pull _____.	Page(s): _____
A magnet's force pulls objects _____.	Page(s): _____
A magnet will not pull _____.	Page(s): _____

What are a magnet's poles?	**Text Evidence**
The poles are the two _____.	Page(s): _____
Two unlike poles _____.	Page(s): _____
Like poles _____.	Page(s): _____

COLLABORATE

Group Discussion Present your answers to the group. Cite text evidence to justify your thinking. Listen to and discuss the group's opinions about your answers.

Write Review your notes. Then write your answer to the Essential Question. Use text evidence to support your answer. Use vocabulary words in your writing.

What are ways we can use magnets?

A can opener _____.

It _____.

There is a magnet in _____.

The magnet holds the door _____.

In the future, magnets _____

_____.

Share Writing Present your writing to the class. Discuss their opinions. Think about what the class has to say. Do they justify their claims? Explain why you agree or disagree. You can say:

I agree with _____ because _____.

I disagree because _____.

165

Write to Sources

pages 158–163

Take Notes About the Text I took notes on the text to answer the question: *What is the author's message about how we use magnets?*

Paul

A magnet is used in a can opener.

A magnet makes a tight seal in a refrigerator.

Magnets have surprising uses.

Toy trains use magnets.

Powerful magnets can move real trains.

166

Write About the Text **I used my notes to write about the author's message.**

Magnets have surprising uses.

Magnets are used in can openers.

They pull the lid off a soup can.

Magnets give a refrigerator a tight

seal. They are used in toy trains.

They can even move real trains!

Magnets are amazing!

TALK ABOUT IT

Text Evidence **Circle** a fact about magnets. What does the fact tell about?

Grammar **Box** the first action verb. What do magnets do? Why does Paul use the present tense in this sentence?

Connect Ideas **Underline** the two sentences about can openers. How can you combine the two sentences?

Your Turn

Answer the question: How do the diagrams on pages 160 and 161 help explain how magnets work?

≫ *Go Digital*
Write your response online. Use your editing checklist.

168

COLLABORATE **Describe what you see in the photograph. In the chart, write what you can see in the sky in the daytime and in the nighttime.**

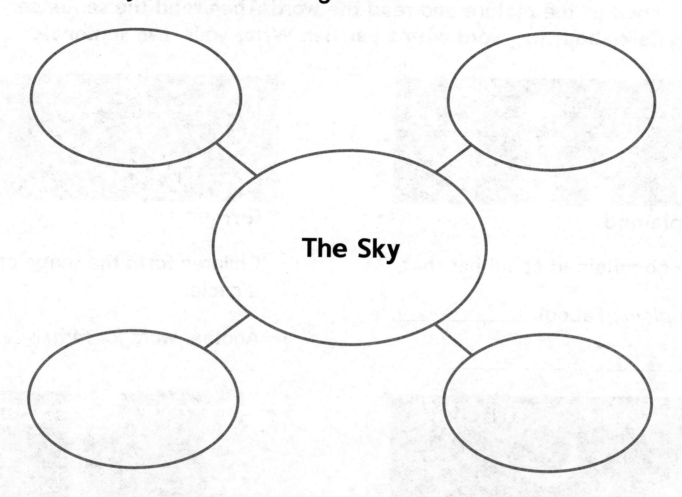

The Sky

Discuss the photograph. Talk about things we can all see in the sky. Use words from the chart. You can say:

A _____ is pointing up _____.

She can see _____ and _____.

More Vocabulary

 Look at the picture and read the word. Then read the sentence.
COLLABORATE Talk about the word with a partner. Write your own sentence.

complained

Elena **complained** about her shirt.

I *complained* about _____

_____ .

crescent

The moon has a **crescent** shape.

A *crescent* shape is _____

_____ .

form

Children **form** the shape of a circle.

Another word for *form* is _____ .

hope

They **hope** to see each other soon.

I *hope* to _____

_____ .

170

poked

The animal **poked** its head out.

The animal *poked* its head out to

_____.

spotted

They **spotted** balloons in the sky.

I *spotted* _____

_____.

Words and Phrases
Contractions: *couldn't, won't*

A contraction is a short way to write two words.

***couldn't* = could not**
We <u>couldn't</u> go outside.

***won't* = will not**
I <u>won't</u> be home today.

Read each sentence. Write the two words for each underlined contraction.

I <u>couldn't</u> find my shoes.

I _____ find my shoes.

The car <u>won't</u> start.

The car _____ start.

>> *Go Digital* **Add these contractions to your New Words notebook. Write a sentence to show the meaning of each word.**

COLLABORATE

① Talk About It

Look at the picture. Read the title. Talk about what you see. Write your ideas.

What does the title tell you about the story?

_____

_____

_____.

What does the illustration show?

_____

_____

_____.

Take notes as you read the text.

Starry Night

Essential Question

? **What can we see in the sky?**

Read about what happens when two girls look for the Big Dipper.

Chris Canga

Josie and Ling were good friends. Ling was happy Josie was her neighbor. Josie was happy Ling lived nearby, too.

Josie and Ling couldn't wait for the school day to end. They **planned** a sleepover at Josie's house. They were going to sleep in a tent in Josie's backyard.

As the class was leaving, Mr. Cortes said, "Your weekend homework is to look at the nighttime sky and explain what you saw on Monday." The class grumbled. "Why the unhappy sounds?" Mr. Cortes asked. "It will be fun looking at the sky at night."

❶ **Specific Vocabulary** Ⓐ Ⓒ Ⓣ

The word *planned* tells about something the characters are going to do. Underline what Josie and Ling planned to do.

❷ **Sentence Structure** Ⓐ Ⓒ Ⓣ

Look at the first sentence in the third paragraph. Underline the words Mr. Cortes says. Box the text that tells when he says this.

❸ **Comprehension**

Why does the class make unhappy sounds?

The class grumbles because

_____

_____

_____.

Text Evidence

1 Specific Vocabulary Ⓐ Ⓒ Ⓣ

Reread the first sentence. The word *outdoors* means "outside." Box how the girls feel to be sleeping outdoors.

2 Comprehension
Sequence

Reread the second paragraph. What does Josie's dad want the girls to do first?

_____

_____

COLLABORATE

3 Talk About It

How do the girls feel about doing their homework now? Circle details that tell you.

The girls arrived at Josie's house and were delighted to be sleeping **outdoors**. Josie said, "I'm so happy that we get to sleep in the tent. It will be lots of fun." Then Ling said, "I'll get the sleeping bags and flashlights. I brought flashlights so we can play games in the tent."

Josie's dad **poked** his head inside the tent. "Girls, it is a good time to do your homework now because it is getting dark," he said. "Awww," they both **complained**. "Dad," said Josie, "do we have to, now?"

"Yes, I already set up the telescope."

Chris Canga

Ling said, "I **hope** this won't take too long." Josie looked up and **spotted** a **crescent** moon. "Did you know the moon's light comes from the sun?" said Josie. "It's funny that it's called moonlight." "Yes," said Ling, who was still thinking about playing in the tent.

Josie's dad smiled at the girls and said, "See the stars in the sky? Those points of bright light can **form** shapes."

"You can see the Big Dipper," he said. "It's a group of stars that look like a giant spoon in the sky."

The Big Dipper

Text Evidence

❶ Comprehension

Sequence

Reread the first paragraph. Draw a box around the first thing the girls see in the sky.

❷ Sentence Structure

In the last sentence in the first paragraph, circle the character the pronoun *who* refers to. Box what Ling is still thinking about.

COLLABORATE

❸ Talk About It

Talk about what Josie's dad teaches the girls. What is the Big Dipper?

_____

_____

_____

_____.

175

❶ Specific Vocabulary Ⓐ Ⓒ Ⓣ

Circle the words that help you understand the meaning of *telescope*.

What does the telescope help Josie see? Underline the word.

❷ Comprehension

Sequence

Who looks through the telescope first?

___

Who has a turn to look through it next? Circle the words that tell you. Underline details that tell what the character sees.

Josie's dad showed her how to look through the **telescope**. "Wow, that's more stars than I ever dreamed of. I never imagined there could be so many."

It was Ling's turn to look. Ling cried out, "I see a bright light moving in the sky!"

"That's a shooting star!" said Josie's dad.

"This is fun," said Ling. "I really enjoy looking at the stars."

Chris Canga

"I think we've seen enough of the nighttime sky," said Josie's dad. "You girls can go play now."

"Aw, Dad, can't we keep looking?" asked Josie. "This is really fun."

"Yes," said Ling. "We have had an adventure already, and we haven't even played in the tent yet!"

"You're right, Ling," said Josie. "This has been one exciting night."

Make Connections

? What did you learn about the nighttime sky after reading this story?

ESSENTIAL QUESTION

Compare what the girls saw in the nighttime sky to what you have seen in the nighttime sky. TEXT TO SELF

Text Evidence

1 Comprehension

Sequence

Reread the first paragraph. Circle what Josie's dad thinks the girls want to do?

2 Sentence Structure A C T

Reread the second sentence in the third paragraph. Box the word that connects the two parts of the sentence. Underline the part that tells what the kids had already.

COLLABORATE

3 Talk About It

What do the girls want to do at the end of the story?

_____

_____

_____ .

Respond to the Text

COLLABORATE

Partner Discussion **Answer the questions. Discuss what you learned in "Starry Night." Write the page numbers where you found text evidence.**

What do Josie and Ling see in the nighttime sky?　　**Text Evidence** 🔍

First, Josie sees _____.　　Page(s): _____

They see a group of stars called _____.　　Page(s): _____

Finally, Ling sees _____.　　Page(s): _____

How does Josie's dad help with their homework?　　**Text Evidence** 🔍

First, he sets up a _____.　　Page(s): _____

Josie's dad explains _____.　　Page(s): _____

He tells Ling _____.　　Page(s): _____

COLLABORATE

Group Discussion **Present your answers to the group. Cite text evidence to justify your thinking. Listen to and discuss the group's opinions about your answers.**

178

Write Review your notes. Then write your answer to the Essential Question. Use text evidence to support your answer. Use vocabulary words in your writing.

> **What can the girls see in the nighttime sky?**
>
> First, Josie looks up and _____
>
> _____. Next, Josie's dad explains _____
>
> _____.
>
> One group of stars is the _____.
>
> Then the girls look through a _____
>
> at many _____. Finally, Ling sees _____
>
> _____ called _____.

Share Writing Present your writing to the class. Discuss their opinions. Think about what the class has to say. Do they justify their claims? Explain why you agree or disagree. You can say:

I agree with _____ because _____.

I disagree because _____.

Write to Sources

pages 172–177

Amelia

Take Notes About the Text I took notes on this story map to respond to the prompt: *Add to the story. Have Ling and Josie tell their class what they saw in the nighttime sky.*

> Josie spots a crescent moon.

⬇

> Dad shows them the Big Dipper. He explains how groups of stars can "form shapes."

⬇

> Josie and Ling see many stars through a telescope.

⬇

> Ling sees a bright light called a shooting star. Josie says it's been an "exciting night."

Write About the Text I used my notes from my story map to add to the story.

Student Model: *Narrative Text*

Ling and Josie speak to their class. Josie says, "First, I saw a crescent moon. Then my dad showed us the Big Dipper. It's a group of stars. It's shaped like a big spoon."

Ling says, "Finally, we saw a bright light move across the sky. It was a shooting star."

Ling and Josie say, "Looking at the night sky is exciting!"

TALK ABOUT IT

COLLABORATE

Text Evidence **Underline** the words Amelia used to show order. Use these words to tell what the girls saw.

Grammar **Circle** the present-tense verb in the first sentence. How do you write this verb to show the past tense?

Condense Ideas **Box** the sentences that describe the Big Dipper. How can you combine them with the word *that*?

Your Turn

COLLABORATE

Write a paragraph that tells what Ling and Josie will do the next time they sleep in Josie's backyard.

>> *Go Digital*
Write your response online. Use your editing checklist.

TALK ABOUT IT

Weekly Concept Ways People Help

? **Essential Question**
How can people help
out their community?

>> *Go Digital*

182

COLLABORATE How do the children help in the neighborhood garden? What are ways you can help in your community? Write your ideas on the chart.

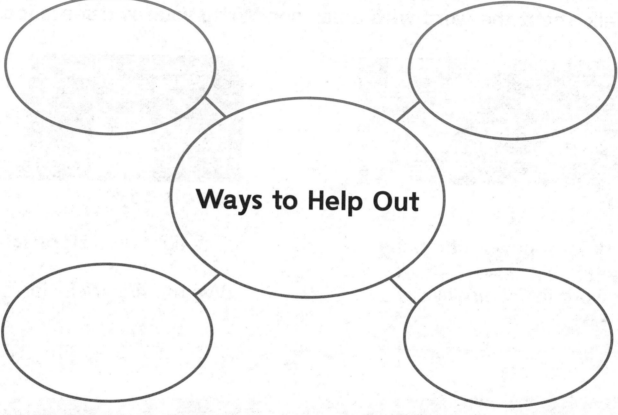

Ways to Help Out

Discuss how the kids help out in the garden. Talk about ways you can help out in the community. You can say:

Kids help _____ in _____.

I can _____.

I think kids can also _____.

More Vocabulary

 Look at the picture and read the word. Then read the sentences. Talk about the word with a partner. Write your own sentence.

company

They work for a power **company**.

Another word for *company* is _____

_____ .

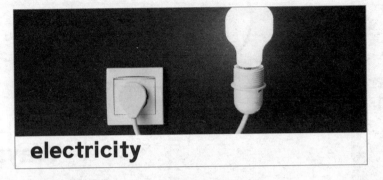

electricity

The light uses **electricity**.

We use *electricity* for _____

_____ .

demands

Mom **demands** we eat our lunch.

Our teacher *demands* _____ .

heat

Zoe **heats** soup for lunch.

In winter, we *heat* _____ .

provided

Helpers **provided** water to runners.

The teacher *provided* _____

_____ to us.

realized

Liz **realized** that she woke up late.

I *realized* that _____

_____ .

Words and Phrases
turn on and *turn into*

Turn on **= to cause to start**
Lara <u>turns on</u> the radio.

Turn into **= to change and become something else**
A tadpole <u>turns into</u> a frog.

Write the correct forms of *turn on* or *turn into* to complete each sentence.

The seed _____ a plant.

Dad _____ the television.

» Go Digital Add the phrases *turn on* and *turn into* to your New Words notebook. Write a sentence to show the meaning of each phrase.

COLLABORATE

1 Talk About It

Look at the photographs. Read the title. Talk about what you see. Write your ideas.

What does this title tell you?

_____

_____

_____.

How do people in a house like this get light?

_____

_____

_____.

Take notes as you read the text.

Lighting Lives

Essential Question

?

How can people help out their community?

Read to learn how one person is helping people in her community.

Independent Picture Service/Alamy (inset) Debby Tewa/Miller Tewa (inset) Nic Taylor/Getty Images

When Debby Tewa was your age, her home had no **electricity**. She could not **flip a light switch** to read at night. She lit a candle. She could not cook on a stove or in a microwave oven. Her family cooked over a fire.

Debby lived in Arizona. When she was ten, she moved to a new home. Her new home had electricity! She could turn on a lamp and use a phone. She liked it!

Debby Tewa lived in a home that had small windows like this one. There was not a lot of light.

Text Evidence

❶ Comprehension
Author's Purpose

Reread the first sentence. What does the author explain about Debby's life at your age?

_____

_____

❷ Specific Vocabulary Ⓐ Ⓒ Ⓣ

Reread the second and third sentences. To *flip a light switch* means "turn on a light." Underline what Debby did for light at night.

❸ Sentence Structure Ⓐ Ⓒ Ⓣ

Reread the last paragraph. A comma separates two parts of the second sentence. Circle the part that tells when Debby moved to a new home with electricity.

187

1 Comprehension

Author's Purpose

Reread the first paragraph. Circle the sentence that explains the meaning of *solar power*. Underline text that explains how sunlight turns into electricity.

COLLABORATE

2 Talk About It

Talk about the company Debbie went to work for. What did Debbie believe about solar power?

_____

_____

_____

As she grew, Debby **realized** she wanted to learn more about solar power. Solar power is electricity that comes from the sun. Solar panels are put on the roof of a building. The sunlight hits these panels and turns the sunlight into electricity.

Debby thought a lot about solar power. Then she had an idea! She was excited. She went to work for a **company** that **provided** solar power to people's homes. She believed it would be a good solution for people who had no electricity. Debby likes solving problems!

Solar panels are now used on many homes.

Debby also thought of people in villages like the one she lived in as a child. The people in these small towns did not have any electricity. Solar power would work well there because there is a lot of sun in Arizona. Debby decided to help these families get solar power.

To get a family started, Debby helps them borrow money from a bank to buy the panels. After they get the money from the bank, they have some time to pay the money back. And the good **news** is there is no cost for using the sun's power!

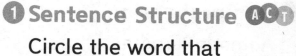

Text Evidence

❶ Sentence Structure Ⓐ Ⓒ Ⓣ

Circle the word that connects the two parts of the third sentence. Box the part that tells why solar power works well in Arizona.

❷ Comprehension
Author's Purpose

Reread the second paragraph. The author explains how Debby helps families borrow money. Circle what people use the money for.

❸ Specific Vocabulary Ⓐ Ⓒ Ⓣ

The *news* can mean "information about something." Underline the good news about using solar energy.

(tl) Ellen McKnight/Alamy

Text Evidence

1 Comprehension

Author's Purpose

Reread the first paragraph. The author describes Debby's work. Underline where Debby travels. Circle what she does there.

2 Sentence Structure

Reread the first sentence in the last paragraph. The word *and* connects two things Debbie does. Circle what she believes in. Box what she insists.

COLLABORATE

3 Talk About It

Why does Debby travel to schools and summer camps?

Debby travels across lands outside cities in Arizona and New Mexico. She travels to the countryside. She helps Hopi and Navajo people get solar power.

Debby believes deeply in her work and insists that families learn about how solar power can help them. They are happy to do what she **demands**. Debby also travels to schools and summer camps to teach Hopi children about solar energy.

Debby helps many Hopi people.

Debby drives her truck **from place to place**. It is lonely with no one riding along. Then she thinks about how exciting it was to use electricity for the first time. Now families can do the things you do without thinking about them. They can **heat** their homes or turn on a light! Debby says she is, "lighting up people's lives."

Make Connections

? How does Debby help her community? ESSENTIAL QUESTION

Talk with a partner about solar power. Could you use it where you live? TEXT TO SELF

Text Evidence

1 Specific Vocabulary ACT

Reread the first sentence. The phrase *from place to place* means "to many places." Box what Debby does from place to place.

2 Sentence Structure ACT

The word *then* connects the third sentence to the text before it. Underline what Debby does when she is lonely driving her truck.

COLLABORATE

3 Talk About It

What does Debby mean when she says she is "lighting up people's lives"?

_____

_____

_____.

Respond to the Text

Partner Discussion Answer the questions. Discuss what you learned about "Lighting Lives." Write the page numbers where you found text evidence.

Why was Debby interested in solar energy?	**Text Evidence**
When Debby was young, _____.	Page(s): _____
Then, Debby moved _____.	Page(s): _____
As Debby grew, she realized _____.	Page(s): _____

How does Debby help people?	**Text Evidence**
Debby teaches _____.	Page(s): _____
Debby travels to _____.	Page(s): _____
Debby helps families borrow _____.	Page(s): _____

Group Discussion Present your answers to the group. Cite text evidence to justify your thinking. Listen to and discuss the group's opinions about your answers.

192

Write Review your notes. Then write your answer to the Essential Question. Use text evidence to support your answer. Use vocabulary words in your writing.

How does Debby help out in her community?

As Debby grew, she realized _____

_____ .

Now, Debby travels the countryside _____

_____ .

She helps people borrow _____

_____ .

Share Writing Present your writing to the class. Discuss their opinions. Think about what the class has to say. Do they justify their claims? Explain why you agree or disagree with their claims.

I agree with _____ because _____ .

I disagree because _____ .

Write to Sources

pages 186–191

Take Notes About the Text I took notes about the text to respond to the prompt: *Do you think Debby's job is important? Why or why not?*

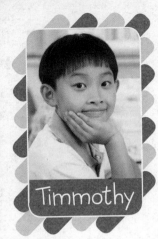

Timmothy

Debby helps families borrow money from banks to buy solar panels.

Debby travels to the countryside to help Hopi and Navajo people.

Debby's Job

Solar panels turn the sun's energy into electricity.

Debby helps people who do not have electricity.

Write About the Text I used my notes to write my opinion of Debby's job.

Debby's job is important. She helps people. She travels to the countryside. She helps people who do not have electricity. Debby helps the families borrow money from a bank. They use the money to buy solar panels. The solar panels turn sunlight into electricity. People can now use electricity for light and other important things.

TALK ABOUT IT COLLABORATE

Text Evidence **Underline** how Debby helps families. How do they get money?

Grammar **Box** two words that name what families buy. What do these things do to sunlight?

Connect Ideas **Circle** the first and second sentences. How can you connect them using the word *because*?

Your Turn COLLABORATE

What do you think is the most important part of Debby's job? Use details from the text in your answer.

>> *Go Digital*
Write your response online. Use your editing checklist.

TALK ABOUT IT

Weekly Concept Weather Alert

? **Essential Question**
How does weather affect us?

>> *Go Digital*

196

What do you see in the photo? Write ways that the weather can affect us in the chart.

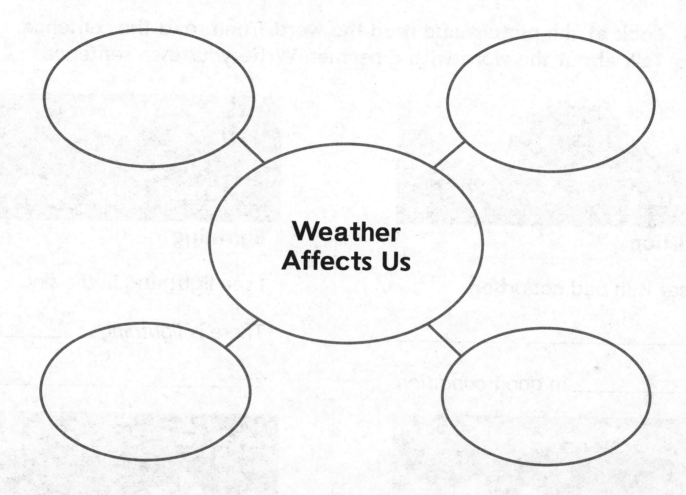

Weather Affects Us

How does the weather affect the children? Discuss how the weather affects you and your family. Use words from the chart. You can say:

The children _____.

My family _____.

More Vocabulary

COLLABORATE

Look at the picture and read the word. Then read the sentence. Talk about the word with a partner. Write your own sentence.

condition

The car is in bad **condition**.

_____

_____ in good *condition*.

drills

Our class has fire **drills**.

We do *drills* because _____

_____.

lightning

I see **lightning** in the sky.

There is *lightning* _____

_____.

repair

The mechanic **repairs** the car.

He *repairs* _____

_____.

spin

A top can **spin** in circles.

A _____ can *spin*.

toss

They **toss** the ball.

Another word for *toss* is _____

_____.

Words and Phrases
more and *most*

More compares two things.
Carmen has <u>more</u> books than Cristina.

Most compares three or more things.
Arlo has the <u>most</u> books in the group.

Most can also mean "almost all."
Jed ate <u>most</u> of the apple.

Write *more* or *most* to complete each sentence.

We won _____ games than we lost.

Our group has the _____ members.

All birds have wings, and _____ birds fly.

>> *Go Digital* Add the words *more* and *most* to your New Words notebook. Write sentences to show their meanings.

(t)rolfo/Flickr RF/Getty Images; (b)Stockbyte/Getty Images

199

COLLABORATE

1 Talk About It

Look at the photograph. Read the title. Talk about what you see. Write your ideas.

What does this title tell you about the text?

_____

_____

_____ .

What is happening in the photograph?

_____

_____

_____ .

Take notes as you read the text.

Tornado!

Essential Question

How does weather affect us?

Read about how tornadoes form and how weather affects our lives.

Wave/Photolibrary

What Is a Tornado?

The sky is dark far away. Something moves down from the clouds. It **spins** across the land. It sounds like a very loud train. A tornado is coming!

A tornado is a spinning cloud. It is shaped like a **funnel**. Its winds can reach 300 miles per hour. That is faster than a race car. The spinning air pulls things up. It can **toss** a car in the air. It can even destroy, or ruin a house. A tornado can be dangerous. It can cause harm to people and places.

When a funnel cloud reaches the ground, it becomes a tornado.

1 Sentence Structure ⒶⒸⓉ

Reread the first paragraph. What spins across the land and sounds like a loud train? Circle the noun that names this thing.

2 Specific Vocabulary ⒶⒸⓉ

A *funnel* is wide on top and thin at the bottom. What has the shape of a funnel?

3 Comprehension
Main Idea and Details

Reread the second paragraph. Underline two details that tell how fast a tornado moves. Box two details that tell how the spinning air can cause harm.

201

Text Evidence

❶ Comprehension
Main Idea and Details

Reread the subhead and first paragraph. Underline the details that tell about thunderstorms. How does a thunderstorm become a tornado?

A tornado is formed when

_____

_____

_____.

❷ Sentence Structure Ⓐ Ⓒ Ⓣ

Reread the second sentence in the last paragraph. The first comma separates parts of the sentence. Circle the part that tells what happens when tornadoes stay on the ground.

How Does a Tornado Form?

A tornado is a kind of weather. Weather is the **condition** of the air. Most tornadoes begin as a kind of weather called a thunderstorm. Thunderstorms are harsh rainstorms with thunder and **lightning**. These rough storms have high winds and heavy rain. When high winds spin and touch the ground, a tornado is born.

Most tornadoes do not stay on the ground for long. When they do, they can cause a lot of damage, or harm. A tornado is a big event!

Tornado Willoughby Owen/Flickr RF/Getty Images

Where Do Most Tornadoes Happen?

More tornadoes happen in the United States than anywhere in the world. Most of them form in the middle part of our country. Scientists think this might be because warm, **wet** air from the Gulf of Mexico crashes with the cool, dry air from Canada. This area is known as Tornado Alley.

Tornadoes can destroy trees, houses, and property.

Stockbyte/Getty Images

❶ Specific Vocabulary Ⓐ Ⓒ Ⓣ

The words warm and cool are antonyms in the third sentence. Circle the antonym for wet in the sentence. Underline what crashes with the warm, wet air from the Gulf of Mexico.

COLLABORATE

❷ Talk About It

Why is the middle part of the country known as Tornado Alley?

_____

_____

_____.

1 Specific Vocabulary A C T

Reread the first paragraph. A *weak* tornado cannot cause as much damage as a strong tornado. Circle what weak tornadoes do.

2 Comprehension
Main Idea and Details

Reread the second paragraph. Box how people know a tornado is coming.

3 Sentence Structure A C T

The word *so* connects two parts of the third sentence. Underline the part that tells why schools provide, or have, tornado drills.

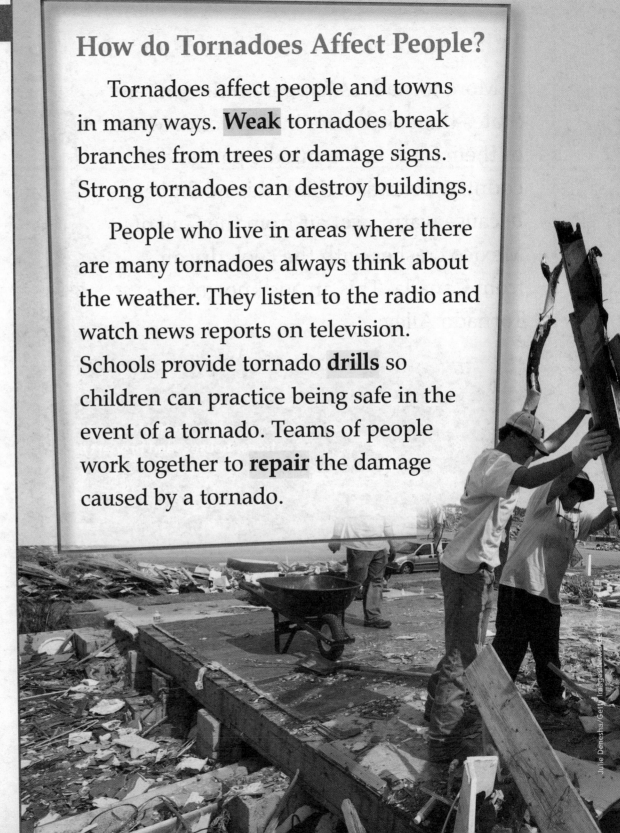

How do Tornadoes Affect People?

Tornadoes affect people and towns in many ways. **Weak** tornadoes break branches from trees or damage signs. Strong tornadoes can destroy buildings.

People who live in areas where there are many tornadoes always think about the weather. They listen to the radio and watch news reports on television. Schools provide tornado **drills** so children can practice being safe in the event of a tornado. Teams of people work together to **repair** the damage caused by a tornado.

How Can You Stay Safe?

There are ways to prevent, or stop, harm during a tornado. News reports use the words tornado warning to give notice that a tornado has been seen. Following safety rules can help everyone stay safe during a tornado!

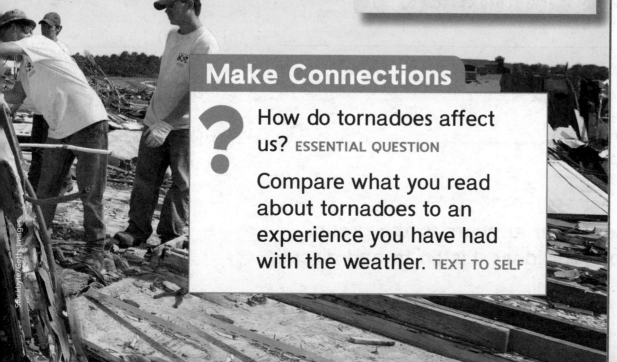

People work together to clean up after a tornado.

Ways to Stay Safe

1. Listen to weather reports.
2. Find shelter in a basement or room without windows.
3. Stay away from windows.
4. Listen to directions from a parent or teacher.

Make Connections

? How do tornadoes affect us? ESSENTIAL QUESTION

Compare what you read about tornadoes to an experience you have had with the weather. TEXT TO SELF

❶ **Comprehension**
Main Idea and Details

When do news reports use the words *tornado warning*?

A tornado warning tells when

_____

_____.

COLLABORATE

❷ **Talk About It**

Look back at the sidebar "Ways to Stay Safe." Talk about the safety rules everyone should follow during a tornado.

Where should you go during a tornado?

_____

_____

_____.

205

Respond to the Text

Partner Discussion Answer the questions. Discuss what you learned about "Tornado!" Write the page numbers where you found text evidence.

How is a tornado born?	Text Evidence 🔍
Most tornadoes begin as a _____.	Page(s): _____
When high winds spin and _____.	Page(s): _____
Most tornadoes happen _____.	Page(s): _____

What harm can tornadoes cause?	Text Evidence 🔍
A tornado can toss _____.	Page(s): _____
Tornadoes can _____.	Page(s): _____
Teams work to repair the _____.	Page(s): _____

Group Discussion Present your answers to the group. Cite text evidence for your ideas. Listen to and discuss the group's opinions.

Write Review your notes. Then write your answer to the Essential Question. Use text evidence to support your answer. Use vocabulary words in your writing.

How do tornadoes affect us?

Tornadoes can _____

_____ .

It is important to watch _____ .

People need to follow _____ .

Teams _____

_____ .

Share Writing Present your writing to the class. Discuss their opinions. Think about what the class has to say. Do they justify their claims? Explain why you agree or disagree with their claims.

I agree with _____ because _____ .

I disagree because _____ .

Write to Sources

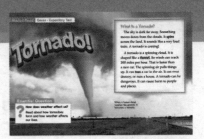

pages 200–205

Andrew

Take Notes About the Text I took notes about the text on this web to respond to the prompt: *How does the author explain what a tornado is?*

The author tells what a tornado looks like and sounds like.

A tornado is a spinning cloud with fast winds.

How does the author explain what a tornado is?

The author describes damage caused by a tornado.

Tornadoes form from thunderstorms.

Eclipse Studios/McGraw-Hill Education

208

Write About the Text I used my notes to write about information in "Tornado!"

Student Model: *Informative Text*

The author of "Tornado!" explains what a tornado is. The author describes what a tornado looks like. The author also tells what it sounds like. A tornado is a spinning cloud and has fast winds. The author explains how one forms from a thunderstorm. The text helped me understand a dangerous kind of weather.

TALK ABOUT IT

Text Evidence **Underline** Andrew's strong ending. What text evidence from the web supports his ending?

Grammar **Box** the subject of the fourth sentence. Make the subject plural. What is the new sentence?

Condense Ideas **Circle** the second and third sentences. How can you combine the ideas into one sentence?

Your Turn

Answer the question: What are some ways tornadoes can affect people? Include text evidence in your answer.

>> Go Digital
Write your response online. Use your editing checklist.

TALK ABOUT IT

Weekly Concept Express Yourself

? Essential Question
How do you
express yourself?

>> *Go Digital*

210

How do the boys express themselves? In the chart, write different ways we can express ourselves.

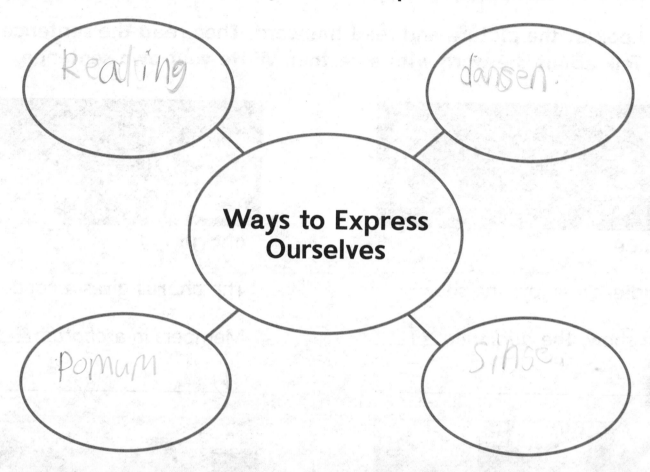

Reading

dansen.

Ways to Express Ourselves

pomum

sihoe.

Talk about how people, such as these boys, express their feelings and share their thoughts. You can say:

I see _____ expressing themselves _____.

One boy is playing the _____. The

other boy is _____.

More Vocabulary

Look at the picture and read the word. Then read the sentence. Talk about the word with a partner. Write your own sentence.

audience

The **audience** enjoys the show.

After a show, the *audience* _uheb_

olso .

beat

The drummers play the **beat**.

Another word for *beat* is _rhythn_

_____ .

chorus

The **chorus** gives a concert.

Members in a *chorus* _sins to_

beacfally togeter .

encourages

The coach **encourages** the team.

A teacher *encourages* _the class._

_____ .

recalls

Grandma **recalls** when she was little.

Another word for *recalls* is _____

_____.

type

A lion is a **type** of big cat.

_____ is a *type* of

_____.

The word *so* shows what happens.
Tomas was tired so he went to bed.

The word *because* shows why something happens.
Tania was happy because her team won.

Write the correct connecting word to complete each sentence.

Tyler goes home _____ he has homework.

Alina was cold _____ she put on a coat.

Write your own sentences using *because* and *so*.

_____

_____

_____

» Go Digital Add the conjunctions *because* and *so* to your New Words notebook. Include your sentences.

(t)KidStock/Blend Images/Getty Images; (b)Pixtal/age fotostock

213

COLLABORATE

1 Talk About It

Look at the picture. Read the title. Talk about what you see. Write your ideas.

Who do you see in the photograph?

_____

_____

_____.

What are they doing?

_____

_____.

Take notes as you read the text.

Essential Question

? How do you express yourself?

Read about how children in a school chorus express themselves.

Carrie Devorah/WENN.com/Newscom

They've Got the Beat!

Some students in New York really **sing their hearts out**! That's because they are in the school **chorus** at Public School 22.

These students from Staten Island had a concert at the White House. They sang at a Hollywood awards show. **Audiences** have clapped and cheered them on. These kids are always asked to return.

How does it feel to sing on stage? "I get nervous singing for a big audience," Brianna Crispino **recalls**. "But when I see the joy on their faces, I get excited."

Brianna Crispino, Public School 22 chorus member

❶ Specific Vocabulary **A C T**

Reread the first paragraph. The words *sing their hearts out* mean "to sing with feeling or to sing well." Circle why the students sing their hearts out.

❷ Sentence Structure **A C T**

Reread the third sentence in the second paragraph. The word *and* connects two actions. Box the two things audiences have done?

❸ Comprehension
Main Idea and Details

Reread the last paragraph. What is the main idea?

Brianna tells how it feels to

_____

_____.

215

1 Specific Vocabulary ⒶⒸⓉ

Reread the first three sentences. To be *divided into* means "separated into parts." Circle the two groups the P.S.22 chorus is divided into.

2 Sentence Structure ⒶⒸⓉ

Reread the next two sentences. The word *so* connects two parts in the last sentence. Underline why it's important for instruments to keep the rhythm.

COLLABORATE

3 Talk About It

Look at the bar graph. Talk about the groups of voices in the adult chorus. What group has the most singers? What group has the fewest singers?

Sounds Good

The P.S.22 chorus is **divided into** two groups. The sopranos sing high notes. The altos sing lower sounds. Instruments like drums sometimes keep the **beat**. It's important to keep the rhythm so they make the right sounds together.

Most adult choruses have four groups of voices. Here's a look at the number of each **type** of voice in one adult chorus from Pennsylvania.

Voices in a Chorus

Bar graph — Number of Singers (vertical axis 0–20) for: Soprano, Tenor, Bass, Alto

Gregg Breinberg, Public School 22 chorus teacher, plays piano to accompany the chorus.

Bebeto Matthews/AP Images

Musical Expression

Being part of the chorus is hard work. The chorus members won't disagree. They practice for three hours each week.

Gregg Breinberg, their teacher, **encourages** the chorus to use movements. They move their hands to show how the songs make them feel. "They have their own movements because nobody feels music the same way," he explains.

The chorus members understand that singing in a chorus is a big job. "We just want to give it our best!" one student says.

Make Connections

? How do the singers in the chorus express themselves? ESSENTIAL QUESTION

How is this the same or different from what you know about singing? TEXT TO SELF

Text Evidence

1 Comprehension
Main Idea and Key Details

What is the main idea of the first paragraph?

Being a member of a chorus

_____

2 Sentence Structure

Reread what Gregg Breinberg explains. Circle the word that connects two parts of the sentence. Underline why the students have their own movements.

COLLABORATE

3 Talk About It

What does one student say about the kids in the chorus?

They _____

_____.

217

Partner Discussion Work with a partner. Discuss what you learned about "They've Got the Beat!" Write the page numbers where you found text evidence.

What is it like to be in the chorus?

Brianna Crispino describes _____.

Page(s): _____

They sing at _____.

Page(s): _____

They move their hands to _____.

Page(s): _____

Text Evidence 🔍

What do the kids do in the chorus?

The chorus has two groups called _____.

Page(s): _____

The kids must keep the rhythm so _____.

Page(s): _____

The kids work hard and _____.

Page(s): _____

Text Evidence 🔍

Group Discussion Present your answers to the group. Cite text evidence for your ideas. Listen to and discuss the group's opinions.

Write Review your notes about "They've Got the Beat!" Then write your answer to the Essential Question. Use text evidence to support your answer. Use vocabulary words in your writing.

How do the singers in the chorus express themselves?

The kids sing at _____

_____.

It is exciting when _____.

The kids move to _____.

The chorus understands _____

_____.

Share Writing Present your writing to the class. Discuss their opinions. Think about what the class has to say. Do they justify their claims? Explain why you agree or disagree.

I agree with _____ because _____.

I disagree because _____.

Write to Sources

Danny

Take Notes About the Text I took notes on this chart to respond to the prompt: *The students in the chorus traveled to different places. Write a paragraph that tells what the kids learned from the travel.*

pages 214–217

They gave a concert at the White House.

The chorus learned from travel.

They sang at a Hollywood awards show.

Audiences clapped and cheered.

Write About the Text I used my notes to explain how the kids learned from travel.

Student Model: *Informative Text*

The kids traveled to many places. They went to the White House. They traveled to a Hollywood awards show. They sang at each place. The students learned about the White House. They learned about show business in Hollywood. The kids learned about new places and different people. Travel teaches many things.

TALK ABOUT IT

COLLABORATE

Text Evidence **Underline** a sentence that uses text evidence from the web. Why is this sentence a key detail?

Grammar **Box** the subject of the first sentence. How can you add the words "in the chorus" to the subject?

Connect Ideas **Circle** the sentences that tell what the students learned. How can you combine the sentences?

Your Turn

COLLABORATE

Why do the kids use rhythm and movement when they sing? Cite text evidence.

>> Go Digital
Write your response online. Use your editing checklist.

Our Life, Our World

The Big Idea

How do different environments make
the world an interesting place?

TALK ABOUT IT

Weekly Concept Different Places

? Essential Question

What makes different parts of the world different?

>> *Go Digital*

COLLABORATE Describe the forest where the family is walking. Describe what it is like where you live. Write your ideas on the chart.

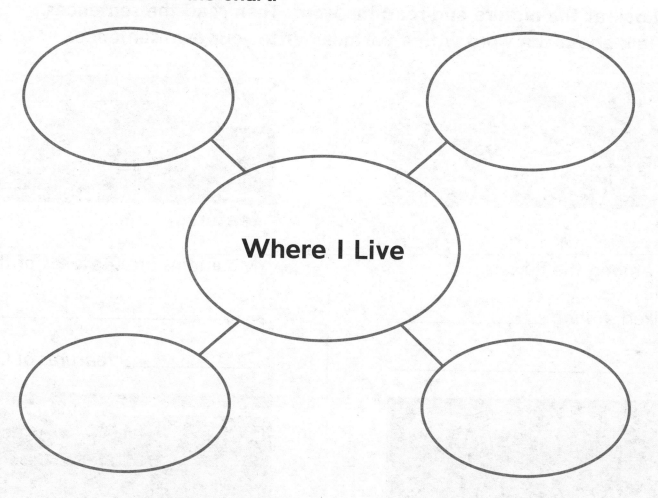

Where I Live

Discuss what your part of the world is like. Use the words from the chart. You can say:

Where I live, there are _____.

It is often _____.

More Vocabulary

Look at the picture and read the word. Then read the sentences.
Talk about the word with a partner. Write your own sentence.

among

We sat **among** the flowers.

We walked *among* _____

_____ .

darkness

He watches stars in the **darkness**.

At the cinema, people watch

_____ in *darkness*.

features

Mountains are **features** of the land.

_____

_____ *features* of California.

frozen

The lake's water is **frozen** into ice.

Water gets *frozen* when _____

_____ .

(tl)SerrNovik/iStock/Getty Images Plus; (tr)Pixtal/age fotostock; (bl)peresanz/iStock/Getty Images Plus/Getty Images; (br)image 100/Alamy

set

The sun will **set** at night.

After the sun *sets,* we _____

_____ .

sunlight

The **sunlight** shines through the trees.

There is *sunlight* _____

_____ .

Words and Phrases
Suffix *-est*

The suffix *-est* compares three or more things.

***tall* + *-est* = tallest**
Dad is the <u>tallest</u> person in our family.

***big* + *-est* = biggest**
Matt picked the <u>biggest</u> apple on the tree.

Read the sentences below. Circle the word that completes each sentence.

The giraffe is the _____ animal at the zoo.   **taller   tallest**

The teacher has the _____ desk in the class.   **bigger   biggest**

>> *Go Digital* **Add the words *tallest* and *biggest* to your New Words notebook. Write a sentence to show the meaning of each word.**

Talk About It

Look at the photograph. Read the title. Talk about what you see. Write your ideas.

What does the title tell you?

_____

_____

_____.

What can you learn about Alaska from the photo?

_____

_____

_____.

Take notes as you read the text.

Alaska
A Special Place

Essential Question

? **What makes different parts of the world different?**

Read to learn what makes Alaska unique.

Where can you find mountains, glaciers, and volcanoes? Alaska is the location you would visit. Alaska has different regions. In each part of the state, there are different **features**.

Land Features

The tallest mountain in the United States is in Alaska. It is called Mt. McKinley. Some people go to Alaska just to climb it.

Alaska also has the biggest glaciers in all of the United States. Glaciers are made when one layer of snow falls on top of another. The snowfall becomes very **thick**. It turns to ice. The growth of a glacier takes many years to form.

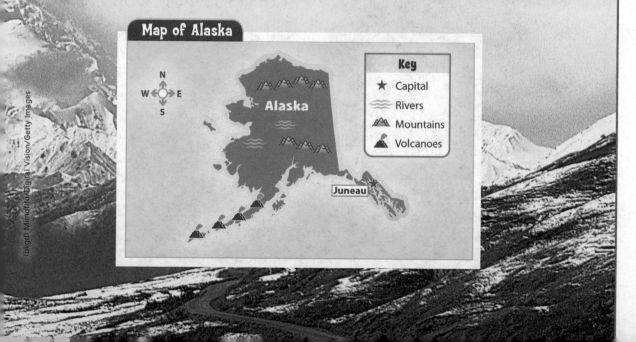

Map of Alaska

Key
★ Capital
〜 Rivers
⩍ Mountains
▲ Volcanoes

Alaska

Juneau

(bkgd) Mimatrio/Digital Vision/Getty Images

1 Sentence Structure A C T

In the first sentence, commas separate three things you can find in Alaska. Circle each of these things, or features of Alaska.

2 Comprehension
Compare and Contrast

Reread the second paragraph. Underline the sentence that compares Mt. McKinley to other mountains in the United States.

3 Specific Vocabulary A C T

The word *thick* tells about the size of the snowfall. What happens to the thick snowfall when it forms a glacier?

_____

_____

_____

Text Evidence

1 Comprehension

Compare and Contrast

Read the first two paragraphs. Why do most people in Alaska live in the south?

It _____

_____ than the Arctic region.

2 Sentence Structure (A)(C)(T)

Look back at the fourth sentence. Circle the commas the separate nouns in the subject. Underline the predicate that tells about these three things.

COLLABORATE

3 Talk About It

Talk about the animals of Alaska. Name three types of bears that live there.

Temperature Changes

Alaska has different temperatures. Northern Alaska is called the Arctic region. The temperatures are much colder than inside your freezer. The ground, lakes, and rivers are almost always **frozen**.

As a result, most people live in the south of Alaska. It is warmer there. Crops grow well in the rich soil there.

Animals

Alaska has many different animals. You may spot a walrus or polar bear **among** the glaciers. You can see a black or brown bear fishing in a river or stream. In another region, you can see a moose or caribou.

Walruses live in shallow waters off the coast of Alaska.

Daylight and Darkness

The seasons are special here, too. In summer, people celebrate the mild temperate weather. These lively people also celebrate the **sunlight** because the Sun does not set for many days. In one village, the Sun doesn't **set** for more than 80 days! You might be in bed and still see the Sun shining.

In winter, the Sun doesn't rise in some places in Alaska. These places have more than 60 days of winter **darkness**. You could have afternoon soccer practice in the dark! You might think this would be eerie, but **Alaskans** don't think this is weird. They are used to the dark winter days.

Alaska is a very interesting place to live!

Steven J. Kazlowski/Alamy; (bkgd) Panoramic Images/Getty Images

Make Connections

What are three things that make Alaska interesting? ESSENTIAL QUESTION

How is where you live different from Alaska? How is it the same? TEXT TO SELF

1 Comprehension
Compare and Contrast

Look back at the first two paragraphs. What two seasons are being compared?

_____

Underline details that tell about daylight and darkness during these seasons.

2 Specific Vocabulary ACT

Alaskans are people who live in Alaska. What can happen in winter that is not eerie or weird for Alaskans?

_____

_____

_____

_____.

231

Respond to the Text

Partner Discussion **Answer the questions. Discuss what you learned about "Alaska: A Special Place." Write the page numbers where you found text evidence.**

	Text Evidence 🔍
What are interesting things to see in Alaska?	
The map shows that Alaska has _____.	Page(s): _____
Alaska has big _____ that are formed when _____.	Page(s): _____
Alaska has many animals, such as _____.	Page(s): _____

	Text Evidence 🔍
What is special about the weather and seasons?	
In the Arctic region, _____.	Page(s): _____
In summer, the Sun _____.	Page(s): _____
But in winter _____.	Page(s): _____

Group Discussion **Present your answers to the group. Cite text evidence to justify your thinking. Listen to and discuss the group's opinions about your answers.**

Write Review your notes. Then write your answer to the
Essential Question. Use text evidence to support your answer.
Use vocabulary words in your writing.

What makes Alaska a special place?

Alaska has different features, such as _____

_____ .

You may see animals, such as _____ .

The seasons in Alaska are special because _____

_____

_____ .

Share Writing Present your writing to the class. Discuss their
opinions. Think about what the class has to say. Do they justify
their claims? Explain why you agree or disagree with their
claims.

I agree with _____ because _____ .

I disagree because _____ .

Write to Sources

Ángela

pages 228–231

Take Notes About the Text I took notes about the text on the web to respond to the prompt: *Why did the author write "Alaska: A Special Place"? Use details from the text in your answer.*

tallest mountain and biggest glaciers in the U.S.

many different kinds of wild animals

Alaska

very cold temperatures in northern Alaska

Sun does not set for days in summer, and in winter it does not rise in places.

Write About the Text I used my notes to write about why Alaska is a special place.

The author explains why Alaska is a special place in our country. Alaska has the tallest mountain. It has the biggest glaciers. Northern Alaska has very cold temperatures. The seasons are interesting in Alaska. There are long summer days. Winter is very dark. The author explains why Alaska is interesting and different from where I live.

TALK ABOUT IT

Text Evidence **Draw a box** around a detail that comes from the notes. Why is this a supporting detail?

Grammar **Underline** the linking verb in the fifth sentence. What two things does the linking verb connect?

Connect Ideas **Circle** the sentences that tell about summer and winter. How can you combine them using the word *but*?

Your Turn

Look at the map on page 229. Write a paragraph that tells why the author used this map.

≫ *Go Digital*
Write your response online. Use your editing checklist.

235

TALK ABOUT IT

? **Essential Question**
How does the Earth change?

>> Go Digital

COLLABORATE Describe what you see in the photograph. What are some things that can change the Earth? Write your ideas on the chart.

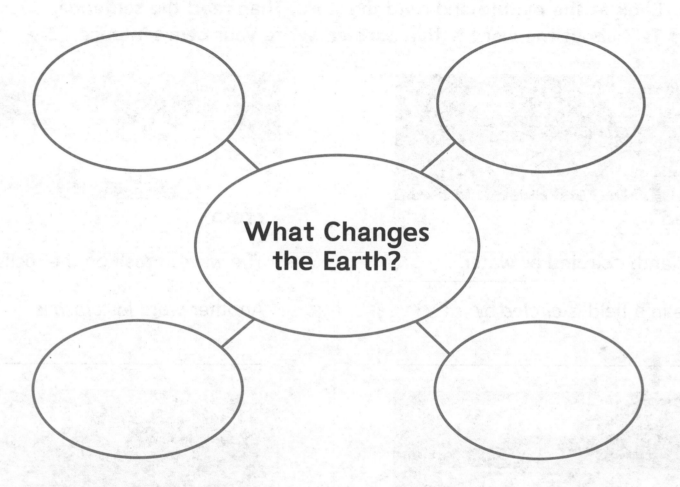

What Changes the Earth?

Discuss what can cause the Earth to change. Use the words from the chart. You can say:

The Earth can change when _____

_____.

More Vocabulary

 Look at the picture and read the word. Then read the sentence.
Talk about the word with a partner. Write your own sentence.

circled

The island is **circled** by water.

A tree in a field is *circled* by

_____.

cliffs

There are **cliffs** above the beach.

The *cliffs* are steep and _____

_____.

crash

The waves **crash** on the rocks.

Another word for *crash* is

_____.

crumble

Sand castles **crumble** in the waves.

_____

_____ can *crumble*.

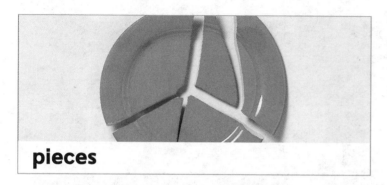

pieces

The plate broke into **pieces**.

I put together the *pieces* of

_____.

weak

The tree has **weak** branches.

The opposite meaning of *weak* is

_____.

Words and Phrases
Prepositions *onto* and *on*

The word *onto* tells where a person or thing goes.
She stepped <u>onto</u> the stage.

The word *on* tells where a person or thing is.
The book is <u>on</u> the shelf.

Read each sentence. Write the word that completes each sentence.

The vase is _____ the table.

       on   onto

The bird flew _____ a tree branch.

       on   onto

>> *Go Digital* Add the prepositions *onto* and *on* to your New Words notebook. Write a sentence to show the meaning of each word.

COLLABORATE

❶ Talk About It

Look at the photograph. Read the title. Talk about what you see. Write your ideas.

What is crashing into the

sand castle? _____

_____

_____.

How does this change the beach?

_____

_____

_____.

Take notes as you read the text.

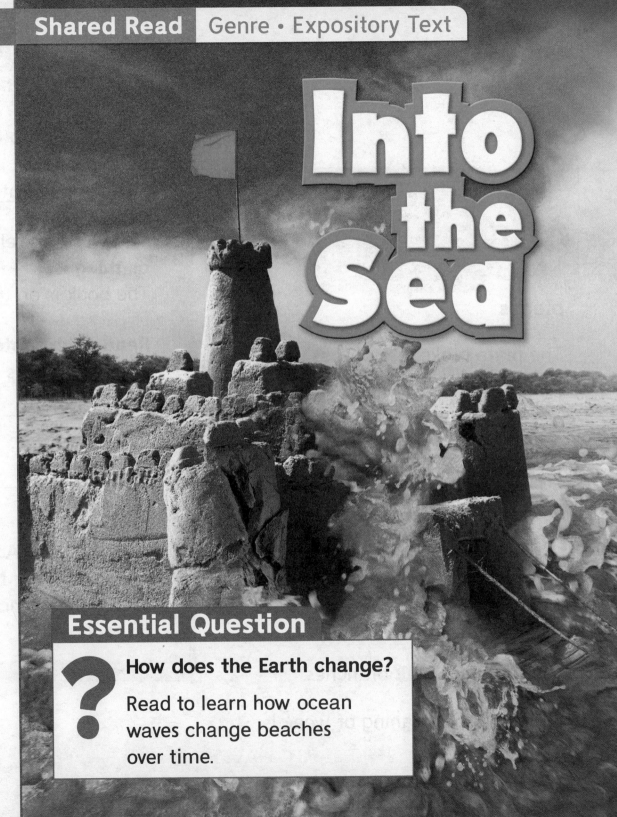

Into the Sea

Essential Question

? **How does the Earth change?**

Read to learn how ocean waves change beaches over time.

What Is Erosion?

Have you ever made a sand castle at the beach? You must pick a good spot for it. If it is too close to the water, waves will quickly wash it away.

Ocean waves and wind can also wash away land. They can change the shape of an island, which is land **circled** by water. When wind and water change the shape of Earth, it is called **erosion**.

Waves are the biggest cause of erosion at the beach. Ocean waves are always active and moving onto the shore. They carry the sand away bit by bit.

Strong waves are one of the properties of big storms. These waves explode as they **crash** onto the beach. Storm waves can move a lot of sand quickly.

Dennis Novak/Photographer's Choice/Getty Images

Text Evidence

❶ Specific Vocabulary Ⓐ Ⓒ Ⓣ

Reread the second paragraph. Underline the words that define *erosion*. What two things cause erosion?

_____

_____

❷ Comprehension
Cause and Effect

Reread the third paragraph. Circle the biggest cause of erosion. Box the sentence that tells how they cause erosion at the beach.

❸ Sentence Structure Ⓐ Ⓒ Ⓣ

Reread the second sentence in the last paragraph. The word *as* tells about two things that happen at the same time. Circle the two things that happen to strong waves.

Before Erosion

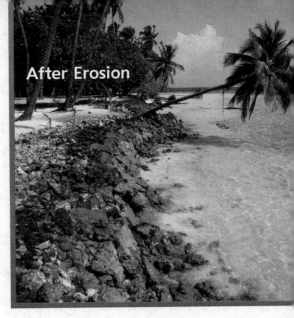
After Erosion

1 Sentence Structure (A)(C)(T)

A comma separates two parts of the third sentence. Underline the part that tells what happens as the beach disappears.

2 Specific Vocabulary (A)(C)(T)

Reread the first sentence in the second paragraph. *Sharp slopes* are steep hills. What happens to rocky cliffs and sharp slopes? Box the word.

3 Comprehension
Cause and Effect

Reread the second paragraph. Underline what makes the top of a cliff weak.

What can this cause?

The cliff can _____

_____ .

Erosion of Beaches

Some people build houses near the ocean. Waves take away the sand between the houses and the sea. As the beach disappears, the water gets closer to houses and other solid buildings on the beach. Some buildings can even be washed away.

Erosion of Rocks

Erosion also happens on steep, rocky **cliffs** or **sharp slopes**. First, waves smash into the bottom of the cliffs. Then they carry away tiny **pieces** of rock. Over time, many small pieces of rock wash away from the bottom of the cliff. This makes the top of the cliff **weak**. The cliff can **crumble** and fall into the sea.

Paul Thompson Images/Alamy

Stopping Erosion

Some local communities work to stop erosion to nearby beaches. These towns have built sea walls of large boulders or rocks.

The rocks are placed in a row in the sea. When waves hit the sea wall, they slow down. Then the waves can't pull sand away.

Some towns make rules about buildings on the beach. New buildings must be far from the water. Then they won't wash away like a sand castle.

Make Connections

? How does beach erosion change the Earth? ESSENTIAL QUESTION

How do the changes from erosion in this selection compare to other changes in nature you have seen? TEXT TO SELF

Text Evidence

1 Sentence Structure **A C T**

Reread the second paragraph. A comma separates two parts of the second sentence. Box the part that tells what happens when waves hit the sea wall.

2 Comprehension
Cause and Effect

Circle what waves can't do because of the sea wall.

COLLABORATE

3 Talk About It

Why do towns build new buildings far from the water?

_____

_____

_____

_____

Respond to the Text

Partner Discussion Work with a partner. Discuss what you learned about "Into the Sea." Write the page numbers where you found text evidence.

What causes erosion?

Beach erosion is caused when _____.

It can result in _____.

Erosion of rocky cliffs happens when _____.

Text Evidence 🔍

Page(s): _____

Page(s): _____

Page(s): _____

What can people do to stop beach erosion?

Some local communities build _____ made of _____.

Sea walls work because _____.

Some towns make rules about _____.

Text Evidence 🔍

Page(s): _____

Page(s): _____

Page(s): _____

Group Discussion Present your answers to the group. Cite text evidence to justify your thinking. Listen to and discuss the group's opinions about your answers.

COLLABORATE

Write Review your notes about "Into the Sea." Then write your answer to the Essential Question. Use text evidence to support your answer. Use vocabulary words in your writing.

How does erosion change the Earth?

Ocean waves _____ .

Beaches can _____ .

Homes can _____ .

Strong waves _____ into the bottom of cliffs

and _____ . The cliffs become

weak and can _____ .

COLLABORATE

Share Writing Present your writing to the class. Discuss their opinions. Think about what the class has to say. Do they justify their claims? Explain why you agree or disagree with their claims.

I agree with _____ because _____ .

I disagree because _____ .

245

Madison

Take Notes About the Text I took notes about the text on this chart to respond to the prompt: *What problem is caused by erosion on the beach?*

pages 240–243

People build houses near the ocean.

⬇

Waves carry sand away from the beach. This causes the beach to slowly disappear.

⬇

Water moves closer to houses and buildings.

⬇

Buildings can wash away.

Write About the Text I used my notes to write about a problem caused by erosion.

Student Model: *Informative Text*

Erosion is a problem at a beach. First, people have built houses on the beach. They are near the ocean. Ocean waves take away sand from the beach. As a result, the beach slowly disappears. The water moves closer to houses. The houses can wash away.

TALK ABOUT IT

Text Evidence **Circle** the detail from the notes that tells what waves take away from the beach. What does this cause?

Grammar **Underline** the predicate in the second sentence. What is the helping verb in the predicate?

Connect Ideas **Box** the fifth and sixth sentences. How can you combine them using the word *and* to connect the ideas?

Your Turn

Write a paragraph that tells how people can use rocks to stop erosion. Include text evidence in your paragraph.

>> Go Digital
Write your response online. Use your editing checklist.

TALK ABOUT IT

Weekly Concept Our Culture Makes Us Special

? Essential Question
How are kids around the world different?

>> *Go Digital*

248

Tell what you know about the game called cricket. How is it the same or different from games you play. How are games around the world the same or different? Write your ideas on the chart.

Same	Different

Describe games that you and your friends like to play. Why are they special to you? Use the words from the chart. You can say:

My friends and I like to play _____

because _____

_____ .

More Vocabulary

COLLABORATE

Look at the picture and read the word. Then read the sentence.
Talk about the word with a partner. Write your own sentence.

carve

The artist **carved** pictures in wood.

I saw _____ *carve*

_____.

includes

My lunch **includes** an apple.

My homework *includes* _____

_____.

leaped

The kids **leaped** in the air.

A _____

can *leap* farther than a person.

pair

A **pair** of birds sat on a branch.

A *pair* is _____

_____ or things.

250

sprinkled

Snow **sprinkled** down on us.

_____

_____ *sprinkled* from the sky.

welcome

We **welcome** people at the door.

Our class *welcomes* _____

_____ .

Words and Phrases
Root Words *celebrate*

celebrate + *-ed* = **celebrated**
We <u>celebrated</u> my birthday last week.

celebrate + *-tion* = **celebration**
My class has a <u>celebration</u> at the end of the year.

Circle the correct word to complete each sentence.

We _____ the New Year together.

celebrated   celebration

We have a _____ for the holiday.

celebrated   celebration

>> *Go Digital* Add the words *celebrated* and *celebration* to your New Words notebook. Write a sentence to show the meaning of each word.

COLLABORATE

1 Talk About It

Look at the picture. Read the title. Talk about what you see. Write your ideas.

What does the title tell you?

_____

_____

_____.

What are the people in the picture doing?

_____

_____

_____.

Take notes as you read the story.

Happy New Year!

Essential Question

?

How are kids around the world different?

Read about a girl celebrating the New Year holiday in the United States and China.

I celebrated the New Year twice in one year. Do you wonder how? I celebrated the **holiday** in the United States and then in China.

On December 31, our city had a celebration to welcome the New Year. This celebration began with a parade. A band played music, and I got my face painted like a lion. Then I watched a man **carve** animals from ice. We were surrounded by fun!

Just before midnight, everyone went to the park. The crowd counted down the last seconds of the old year. Then came my favorite part, the thing I like most. Pop! Pop! Pop! Fireworks like a shower of colorful lights **sprinkled** down from the sky.

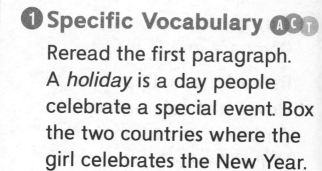

Text Evidence

❶ Specific Vocabulary Ⓐ Ⓒ Ⓣ

Reread the first paragraph. A *holiday* is a day people celebrate a special event. Box the two countries where the girl celebrates the New Year.

❷ Sentence Structure Ⓐ Ⓒ Ⓣ

Reread the third sentence in the second paragraph. Circle the word that connects two parts of the sentence. Underline the part that describes what the girl does.

❸ Comprehension

Box two details in the second paragraph that explain why the girl writes, "We were surrounded by fun!" In the third paragraph, underline the text that tells about the girl's "favorite part."

253

1 Comprehension

Compare and Contrast

Reread the first paragraph. How is the celebration in China different from in the United States?

_____

_____

_____

2 Specific Vocabulary Ⓐ🅒🅣

When something is *interesting,* you like to learn about it. Box an interesting custom the girl learns about.

3 Sentence Structure Ⓐ🅒🅣

Reread the last sentence. The word *and* connects two verbs. Box each thing the firecrackers do in the sky.

Then my family took a plane to China. A plane is huge and travels over the ocean like a whale in the sky. We celebrated Chinese New Year with Grandma. This celebration is different than in the United States. It lasts for fifteen days, not just one night. After we arrived, Grandma surprised me with new red clothing. She said red brings good luck.

On New Year's Eve, we went to Grandma's house. I learned many **interesting** Chinese customs. One custom is to have a family dinner that **includes** tasty dumplings. Then we stepped outdoors to watch a big parade. At the end, a rainbow of firecrackers snapped and popped in the sky!

Later that week we watched the Chinese lion dance. I'd never seen anything like it. Each **pair** of dancers wore a **fancy** lion costume made of cloth as yellow as the Sun. The dancers **leaped** through the air and did amazing tricks!

We went to the Lantern Festival on the last day of Chinese New Year. The full moon hung like a balloon in the dark sky. Everyone made paper lanterns that lit up the night.

The two celebrations were different. They were the same, too. They had one thing in common. They were both exciting family celebrations to **welcome** the New Year!

Susan Swan

Make Connections

? How is the New Year celebration in China different from the celebration in the United States? ESSENTIAL QUESTION

Compare the New Year's celebrations in the story to how you and your family celebrate the New Year. TEXT TO SELF

1 Specific Vocabulary A C T

The word *fancy* means "decorated, or not plain." Underline the words that tell what the girl says is fancy.

COLLABORATE

2 Talk About It

Talk about what happens at the Lantern Festival. What does everyone make at the festival?

3 Comprehension
Compare and Contrast

Reread the last paragraph. What do both celebrations have in common?

Both are _____

_____

_____.

Respond to the Text

Partner Discussion Answer the questions. Discuss what you learned about "Happy New Year!" Write the page numbers where you found text evidence.

How does the girl celebrate in the United States?

Text Evidence 🔍

The celebration begins with _____. Page(s): _____

The girl watches a man _____. Page(s): _____

Just before midnight, everyone _____. Page(s): _____

How does she celebrate in China?

Text Evidence 🔍

On New Year's Eve, the family _____. Page(s): _____

The celebration is different because _____. Page(s): _____

Later in the week, the family _____. Page(s): _____

Group Discussion Present your answers to the group. Cite text evidence to justify your thinking. Listen to and discuss the group's opinions about your answers.

256

COLLABORATE

Write Review your notes. Then write your answer to the Essential Question. Use text evidence to support your answer. Use vocabulary words in your writing.

Compare the New Year celebrations in the two countries.

In the United States, _____

_____.

In China, _____

_____.

Both celebrations _____

_____.

COLLABORATE

Share Writing Present your writing to the class. Discuss their opinions. Think about what the class has to say. Do they justify their claims? Explain why you agree or disagree with their claims.

I agree with _____ because _____.

I disagree because _____.

Write to Sources

pages 252–255

Kevin

Take Notes About the Text I responded to the prompt: *Write a letter from the girl to her grandmother. The girl thanks Grandma for the New Year's Eve celebration in China.*

family dinner with tasty dumplings

New Year's Eve with Grandma

big parade

rainbow of firecrackers

REB Images/Blend Images/Getty Images

258

Write About the Text I used my notes to write a thank-you letter to Grandma.

Student Model: *Narrative Text*

Tuesday, February 12

Dear Grandma,

Thank you for the fun New Year's Eve celebration. I loved the family dinner. I ate tasty dumplings. I liked the dragon in the parade. It was big and colorful. The firecrackers looked like a rainbow! I had a good time. Thank you very much.

Love,

Your granddaughter

TALK ABOUT IT

COLLABORATE

Text Evidence **Circle** a detail that comes from the notes. How is it a supporting detail?

Grammar **Draw a box** around the sentence about dumplings. What verb is the past tense of *eat*?

Connect Ideas **Underline** the sentences that tell about the dragon. How can you combine them using the word *because*?

Your Turn

COLLABORATE

Write a letter from the girl to a friend. Describe the lion dance and Lantern Festival. Include text evidence.

>> *Go Digital*
Write your response online. Use your editing checklist.

COLLABORATE

Why do you think the beetle has such bright colors? What are things in nature that you have wondered about? Write your questions about nature on the chart.

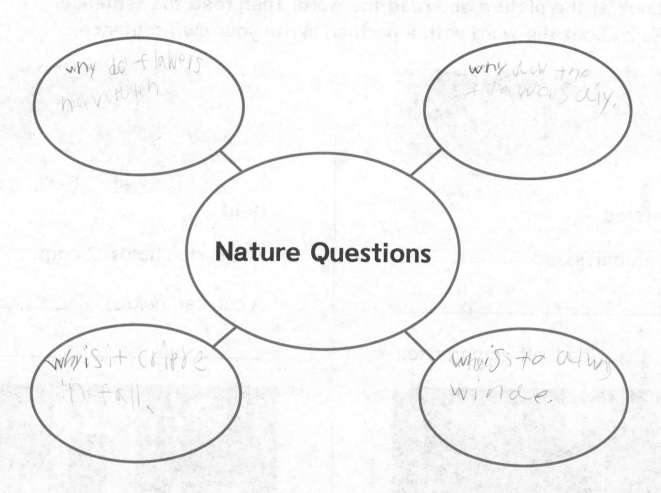

why do flowers navtuth

why dow the flowors diy.

Nature Questions

why is it criepe in fall.

whaiss to alwy winde.

Discuss your questions about nature. Use the words from the chart. You can say:

I wonder why _____.

It could be because _____.

More Vocabulary

Look at the picture and read the word. Then read the sentence. Talk about the word with a partner. Write your own sentence.

embarrassed

Leo felt **embarrassed**.

I _twas dowing wa bakfip_

bat ɫ got and felt *embarrassed*.

guest

We asked our **guest** to come inside.

I was a *guest* at _the Allins._ _____.

hold

The carton **holds** 12 eggs.

A cup can *hold* _100 galins_

of warter. _____.

polite

It is **polite** to hold open the door.

It is *polite* to _do evrething to_

be polite wen we eat
proplle

262

(tl)Sappington Todd/BLOOMimage/Getty Images; (tr)Mark Steinmetz/McGraw-Hill Education; (bl)Huntstock/Getty Images; (br) Summer Derrick/E+/Getty Images

raced

The kids **raced** to catch the bus.

I *raced* to get ___my mom won___

___sh left me at th___.

___school.___

remain

Our desks **remain** at school.

My ___mom___ remains

at home.

Words and Phrases
Root Words *large*

en- + large = enlarge
They added a room to <u>enlarge</u> the house.

large + -er = larger
The dog is <u>larger</u> than the family's cats.

large + -est = largest.
The dog is the family's <u>largest</u> pet.

**Write *enlarge*, *larger*, or *largest*
to complete each sentence.**

We can _____ the picture so we
can all see it.

The elephant is the _____ animal
at the zoo.

My feet are _____ than my little
sister's feet.

>> Go Digital Add the words *enlarge,*
larger, and *largest* to your New Words
notebook. Write a sentence to show the
meaning of each word.

(t)Comstock/Stockbyte/Getty Images; (b)ssuni/E+/Getty Images

263

COLLABORATE

❶ Talk About It

Look at the picture. Read the title. Talk about what you see. Write your ideas.

What does the title tell you?

_____

_____

_____

_____.

What are the characters doing?

_____

_____

_____

_____.

Take notes as you read the story.

Why the Sun and Moon Live in the Sky

Essential Question

? **How can we understand nature?**

Read about how the Sun and the Moon ended up in the sky.

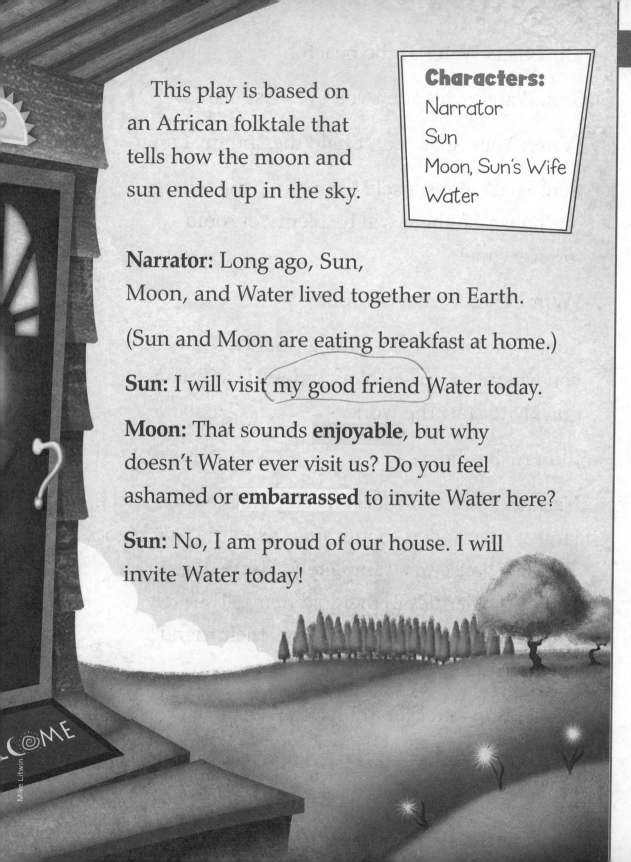

This play is based on an African folktale that tells how the moon and sun ended up in the sky.

Characters:
Narrator
Sun
Moon, Sun's Wife
Water

Narrator: Long ago, Sun, Moon, and Water lived together on Earth.

(Sun and Moon are eating breakfast at home.)

Sun: I will visit my good friend Water today.

Moon: That sounds **enjoyable**, but why doesn't Water ever visit us? Do you feel ashamed or **embarrassed** to invite Water here?

Sun: No, I am proud of our house. I will invite Water today!

Mike Litwin

❶ **Sentence Structure** Ⓐ Ⓒ Ⓣ

Reread what the Narrator says. Box the phrase that tells when the play takes place. Circle the play's characters.

❷ **Comprehension**
Theme

Read the first sentence Sun says. Circle the words he uses to describe Water.

❸ **Specific Vocabulary** Ⓐ Ⓒ Ⓣ

Reread what Moon says next. The word *enjoyable* describes something you are able to enjoy, or something fun. What does Moon think sounds *enjoyable*?

Moon thinks a visit with

____Water____ sounds enjoyable.

Text Evidence

① Talk About It

Talk about why Water cannot visit. How will Sun and Moon solve this problem?

They will ___They will make___ ___the house___.

② Comprehension
Theme

Reread what the Narrator says. Box what Sun and Moon do to make their home larger. Circle how they feel about it.

③ Specific Vocabulary ⒶⒸⓉ

Look back at the Narrator's third sentence. Circle the words with the same meaning as *completely different*. Underline what is completely different from their old home.

266

(Sun visits Water at the beach.)

Sun: Water, why don't you ever visit us?

Water: Your house can't **hold** me and my family.

Sun: That's nonsense! Moon and I will enlarge our house, so there will be plenty of room for everyone!

Water: Then I will visit you.

Sun: Wonderful! Please holler loudly, so I hear you when you arrive. Now I must dash home quickly to start the work.

(Sun rushes home.)

Narrator: Sun and Moon **raced** to make their home larger. They added rooms and raised the roof higher. The new house was **completely different** and had no similarities to their old home. They felt it was a victory, or a win, for now their friend could visit.

Water: Sun and Moon, I have arrived!

Sun: Isn't this the largest home you've seen?

Moon: Sun, it's not **polite** to brag, so please don't boast to our **guest**. Water, come inside.

Narrator: Water splashed through the door carrying colorful fish, frogs, and crabs. As the water began to rise, Sun and Moon climbed onto furniture. Then they scrambled onto the roof.

Sun: Moon, I'm not sure about the wisdom of inviting Water. Perhaps this wasn't a smart idea!

Moon: No, Sun, it was the right thing to do but we must fly to safety!

Narrator: Sun and Moon flew to the sky, where they **remain** today and still shine down on Water.

Make Connections

What does this folktale explain about nature? ESSENTIAL QUESTION

How is this story different from what you know about the Sun and Moon? TEXT TO SELF

Text Evidence

1 Sentence Structure A C T

Reread the Narrator's second sentence. Circle the part of the sentence that tells when Sun and Moon climb onto their furniture.

2 Comprehension
Theme

Why does Moon say inviting Water "was the right thing to do"?

_____

_____

COLLABORATE

3 Talk About It

Discuss why Water's visit causes Sun and Moon to fly to the sky.

Mike Litw

Respond to the Text

Partner Discussion Answer the questions. Discuss what you learned about "Why the Sun and Moon Live in the Sky." Write the page numbers where you found text evidence.

	Text Evidence 🔍
Why do Sun and Moon ask Water to visit?	
Moon asks Sun _____.	Page(s): _____
Sun invites Water but Water says _____.	Page(s): _____
Sun and Moon then _____.	Page(s): _____

	Text Evidence 🔍
What happens when Water visits Sun and Moon?	
Water splashed through the door with _____.	Page(s): _____
The water rises and _____.	Page(s): _____
Finally, Sun and Moon _____.	Page(s): _____

Group Discussion Present your answers to the group. Cite text evidence to justify your thinking. Listen to and discuss the group's opinions about your answers.

268

Write Review your notes. Then write your answer to the
Essential Question. Use text evidence to support your answer.
Use vocabulary words in your writing.

> **What does this play explain about nature?**
>
> Long ago, _____
>
> _____.
>
> Sun and Moon enlarged their house _____
>
> _____.
>
> When Water came, _____
>
> _____.

Share Writing Present your writing to the class. Discuss their
opinions. Think about what the class has to say. Do they
justify their claims? Explain why you agree or disagree.

I agree with _____ because _____.

I disagree because _____.

Write to Sources

Lily

Take Notes About the Text **I took notes about the text on this chart to respond to the prompt:** *Should Sun have invited Water to visit? Use details from the text in your opinion.*

pages 264–267

Water says that Sun's house can't hold him and his family.

↓

Sun and Moon make their home larger.

↓

Water, fish, frogs, and crabs fill the house.

↓

Sun and Moon fly to the sky to safety.

Write About the Text I used my notes about the drama to write my opinion.

Student Model: *Opinion*

It was not a good idea to invite Water to visit. Water told Sun that he couldn't fit in the house. Sun needed to listen. Instead, Sun and Moon made their house bigger. Then Water filled the house. Fish, frogs, and crabs filled the house. Sun and Moon had to fly to the sky for safety. Sun and Moon now live in the sky, so it was not a good idea to invite Water to visit.

TALK ABOUT IT

COLLABORATE

Text Evidence **Underline** a detail from the notes that supports the opinion. Why does it support Lily's opinion?

Grammar **Box** the sentence that tells what Sun and Moon did to their house. What verb is the past tense of *make*?

Condense Ideas **Circle** the sentences that tell what filled the house. How can you combine the ideas into one sentence?

Your Turn

COLLABORATE

You invite Water to your home. Is this a good or bad idea? Use text evidence in your answer.

≫ Go Digital
Write your response online. Use your editing checklist.

Weekly Concept Poems About Nature

? **Essential Question**

What excites us about nature?

>> *Go Digital*

272

COLLABORATE

Describe the whale jumping out of the water. Why is it exciting? What do you see in nature that excites you? Write your ideas on the chart.

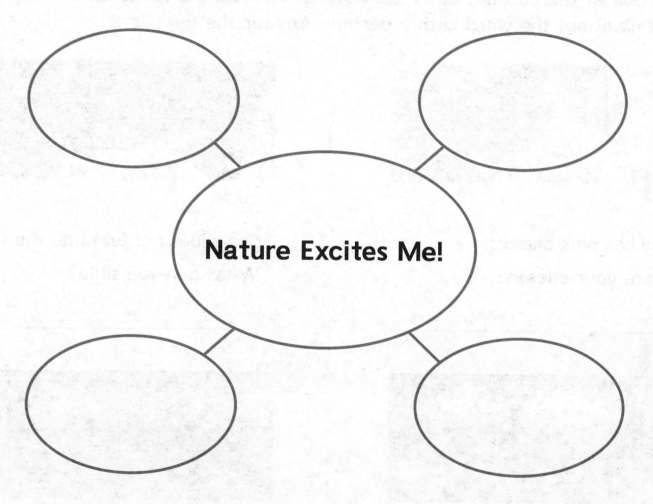

Nature Excites Me!

Discuss something in nature that excites you. Use the words from the chart. You can say:

_____ excites me because _____

_____.

More Vocabulary

Look at the picture. Read the word. Then read the sentences.
Talk about the word with a partner. Answer the question.

cheek

The baby has pink **cheeks**.

Where are your cheeks?

_____

slide

She **slides** her feet into the shoes.

What can you slide?

_____

crunch

The leaves **crunch** under our feet.

What other things crunch?

_____

smooth

The floor is **smooth**.

What things are smooth?

_____

Poetry Terms

alliteration

The words *dog* and *dig* have **alliteration**. They start with the same sound.

The **dog** **digs** in the **dirt**.

simile

A **simile** compares two different things with the words *like* or *as*.

The **snow** is <u>like</u> milk.

The **snow** is <u>as</u> white <u>as</u> milk.

repetition

Repetition repeats the same word or phrase.

Yes! Yes! Yes, they like it.

COLLABORATE

Work with a partner. Make up a simile and use alliteration. Use the words below.

Simile:

eyes   ocean

Lionel's _____ are as blue as the

_____.

Alliteration:

brown   bounce ball

I _____ a big _____

_____.

❶ Literary Element

Simile

Reread line 3. Circle the word that shows there is a simile. What two things does the poet compare?

_____

_____

❷ Literary Element

Alliteration

Circle words with the same beginning sound as *snow* in line 4.

❸ Specific Vocabulary ⒶⒸⓉ

To *ruin* means "to harm or damage." How does the poet feel when she walks through snow?

_____

_____.

Snow Shape

Essential Question

? **What excites us about nature?**

Read how poets describe things in nature.

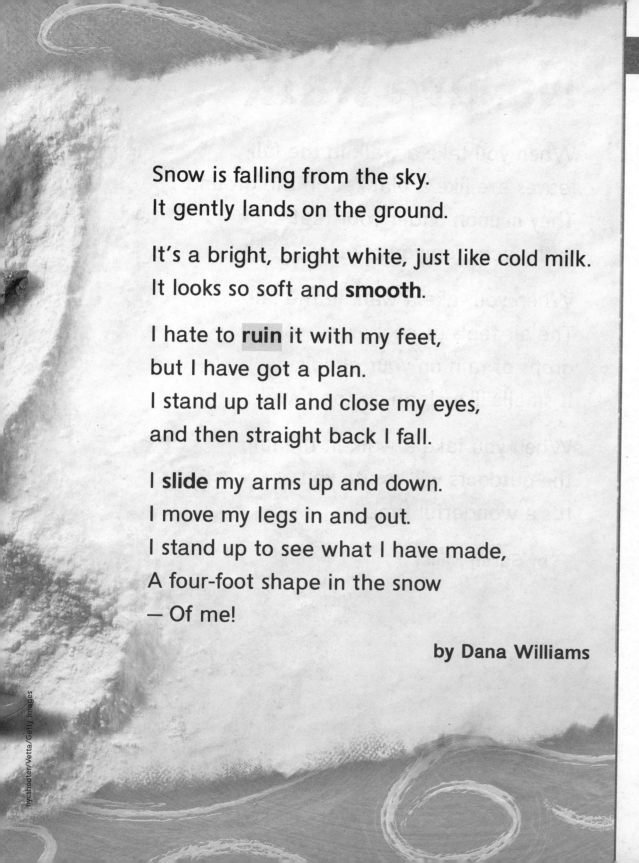

Snow is falling from the sky.
It gently lands on the ground.

It's a bright, bright white, just like cold milk.
It looks so soft and **smooth**.

I hate to **ruin** it with my feet,
but I have got a plan.
I stand up tall and close my eyes,
and then straight back I fall.

I **slide** my arms up and down.
I move my legs in and out.
I stand up to see what I have made,
A four-foot shape in the snow
— Of me!

by Dana Williams

 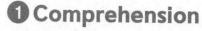
❶ Comprehension
Theme

The poet believes snow is pretty and fun to play in. Underline details that describe the poet playing in the snow.

COLLABORATE

❷ Talk About It

What does the poet make in the snow?

_____

_____

_____

1 Literary Element

Simile

What does the poet compare leaves in the fall to?

_____

_____

COLLABORATE

2 Talk About It

Discuss how the poet describes the air in fall. Circle words that describe how it feels. Box what it smells like.

3 Comprehension

Theme

Read the last three lines. Underline details that tell how the poet feels about taking a walk in the fall.

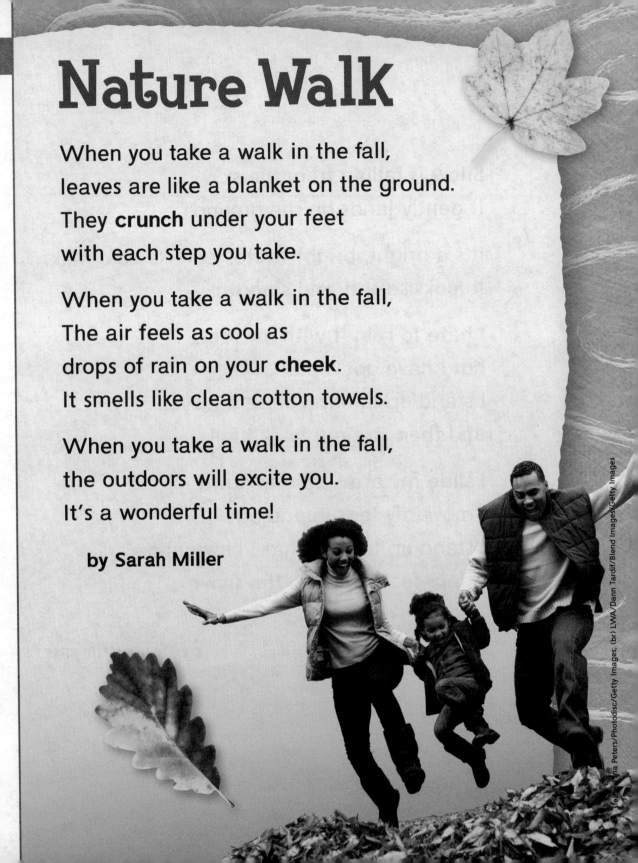

Nature Walk

When you take a walk in the fall,
leaves are like a blanket on the ground.
They **crunch** under your feet
with each step you take.

When you take a walk in the fall,
The air feels as cool as
drops of rain on your **cheek**.
It smells like clean cotton towels.

When you take a walk in the fall,
the outdoors will excite you.
It's a wonderful time!

by Sarah Miller

In the Sky

Outdoors on a clear day,
look up in the sky.
What do you see there?
Look! I see a **giant** polar bear.
Look! I see a pale flower growing.
Look! I see a buffalo and her baby.
Wait...it's changing.
Now I see a cowboy on his horse
Galloping, galloping across the sky.
I wonder where he'll ride?

by Juanita Marco

Make Connections

? Talk about how nature excites the poet of each poem. ESSENTIAL QUESTION

Which poem do you like the most? How does it excite you about nature? TEXT TO SELF

Text Evidence

❶ Literary Element
Repetition

Reread lines four, five, and six. What words does the poet repeat? Box the words.

❷ Specific Vocabulary Ⓐ Ⓒ Ⓣ

The word *giant* means "very large." Circle the giant thing the poet sees.

COLLABORATE

❸ Talk About It

Talk about the different things the poet sees in the sky. What does she wonder about at the end?

_____

_____

_____

279

Respond to the Text

Partner Discussion Answer the questions. Discuss what you learned about "Snow Shape." Write the line numbers where you found text evidence.

What is exciting about nature on a snowy day?

Text Evidence 🔍

Snow falls _____.   Line(s): _____

It is bright _____.   Line(s): _____

It looks _____.   Line(s): _____

What does the poet do in the snow?

Text Evidence 🔍

The poet stands up _____.   Line(s): _____

She slides _____.   Line(s): _____

She makes _____.   Line(s): _____

COLLABORATE

Group Discussion Present your answers to the group. Cite text evidence to justify your thinking. Listen to and discuss the group's opinions about your answers.

Write Review your notes about "Snow Shape." Then write your answer to the Essential Question. Use text evidence to support your answer. Use vocabulary words in your writing.

What excites the poet about snow?

The poet describes how snow _____

_____.

She compares the _____ color of snow to _____.

She describes how it looks _____.

Then she _____ and makes

_____.

Share Writing Present your writing to the class. Discuss their opinions. Think about what the class has to say. Do they justify their claims? Explain why you agree or disagree with their claims.

I agree with _____ because _____.

I disagree because _____.

Write to Sources

Ryan

Take Notes About the Text I took notes on this chart to respond to the prompt: *Does the simile in "Snow Shape" work well or not? Explain why.*

pages 276–279

The word "like" is used to compare two things.

Snow is compared to milk.

"It's bright, bright white, just like cold milk."

Both snow and milk are cold.

Both snow and milk are bright white.

Write About the Text I used my notes to write my opinion about a simile.

A simile compares two different things. A simile uses the words "like" or "as." The author wrote that snow is "bright, bright white, just like cold milk." This simile works well. It uses the word "like." It compares snow and milk. It is good to compare snow and cold milk because both are cold and white.

COLLABORATE

TALK ABOUT IT

Text Evidence Underline words from the poem in Ryan's paragraph. What word tells you this is an example of a simile?

Grammar Circle the last sentence. How can Ryan use the word *bright* to make this statement more descriptive?

Condense Ideas Box the two sentences that explain what the simile does. How can you combine the sentences?

Your Turn

COLLABORATE

What simile in "Nature Walk" do you like best? Explain your opinion.

>> *Go Digital*
Write your response online. Use your editing checklist.

Let's Make a Difference

The Big Idea

How can people make a difference?

TALK ABOUT IT

Weekly Concept Being a Good Citizen

? **Essential Question**
What do good citizens do?

>> *Go Digital*

COLLABORATE How are the girls being good citizens? What are rights that every citizen has? What are some ways that you can be a good citizen? Write your ideas on the web.

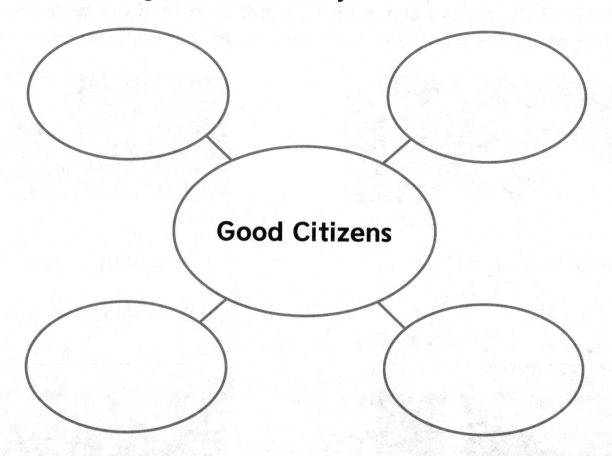

Good Citizens

Discuss ways that you are a good citizen. What are some other things that you can do to be a good citizen? Use the words from the web. You can say:

I am a good citizen when I _____.

I can also _____.

More Vocabulary

COLLABORATE

Look at the picture and read the word. Then read the sentence. Talk about the word with a partner. Write your own sentence.

advice

Dad gives **advice** when I have a problem.

_____ is someone who gives me good *advice*.

claiming

She is **claiming** her bag.

People *claim* something because _____.

duty

It is our **duty** to follow the rules.

It is my *duty* to _____

_____.

equipment

Slides are **equipment** at a playground.

A _____ is my favorite playground *equipment*.

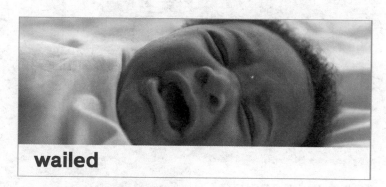

upset

Jenny was **upset** about going to bed.

I feel *upset* when _____

_____.

wailed

The baby **wailed** because he was hungry.

Another word for *wailed* is _____

_____.

Words and Phrases
Whatever and *Whenever*

whatever = anything or everything that
I can choose <u>whatever</u> I want on the menu.

whenever = anytime or every time that
*<u>Whenever</u> my sister picks the game, we
play hide-and-seek.*

**Read the sentences below. Write the
word that best completes each sentence.**

You can use _____ color you want.

whatever   whenever

Friends can help _____ you

have a problem.

whatever   whenever

>> *Go Digital* Add the words *whatever*
and *whenever* to your New Words
notebook. Write a sentence to show the
meaning of each word.

289

COLLABORATE

1 Talk About It

Look at the picture. Read the title. Talk about what you see. Write your ideas.

What does the title tell you?

_____

_____

_____

_____ .

What are the characters doing?

_____

_____

_____ .

Take notes as you read the story.

A Difficult Decision

Essential Question

? **What do good citizens do?**

Read about a boy who chooses to be a good citizen.

My best friend Paul and I were excited to go to the park after school. The park had a new fort. The Parks Department let the kids choose what kind of **equipment** to build, and the fort got the most votes. After school, Mom and I met Paul and his dad at the park.

Paul and I raced to the top of the tower. "I win. I'm the champion," I shouted. "Look, Paul! Someone left the newest GameMaster here. It's mine now!"

Paul raised his eyebrows and looked **thoughtful**. "Wyatt, you cannot keep that GameMaster," he said. "You have a responsibility to return it. It is your **duty**!"

I asked, "Haven't you ever heard the saying, 'finders keepers, losers weepers'? I have rights. I found it, so I am **claiming** it."

Daniel Griffo

1 Comprehension
Point of View

Reread the second paragraph. The character Wyatt is telling the story. Circle the sentence that shows Wyatt's point of view about finding the game.

2 Specific Vocabulary ⒶⒸⓉ

Paul looks *thoughtful* because he thinks seriously about what Wyatt said. Underline what Paul thinks Wyatt should do with the game.

3 Sentence Structure ⒶⒸⓉ

Read the last sentence. Box the word that connects two parts of the sentence. Circle the part that tells why Wyatt is claiming the game.

291

Text Evidence 🔍

1 Talk About It

Reread the first paragraph. Underline how Wyatt is a good citizen at school. Discuss why Paul tells him this.

2 Sentence Structure (A C T)

Reread the second paragraph. Circle the words that show Paul is still speaking.

3 Comprehension
Point of View

Reread the third paragraph. Wyatt knows Paul is right. Why does Wyatt no longer want to keep the game?

_____

_____

_____.

"You can do whatever you want, Wyatt, but you know it's wrong to keep it," Paul said. Then he added, "Whenever there are issues like this at school, you're the one who helps solve the problems. Now you aren't taking your own **advice**."

Then Paul added, "I volunteered my thoughts. If you don't want to take the help I offered, there's nothing I can do."

Paul was right. I couldn't keep the game because it wasn't mine. The person who lost it would be **upset**. I cleared my throat and said in my best deep voice, "I've determined that you're right!"

"I'm delighted you decided to do the right thing," said Paul.

We told my mother what happened. She walked around the park with us so we could try to find the owner of the game. Soon we saw a boy and his Mom looking for something. He looked hopeless, and he burst into tears when we asked him if the game was his. "Yes," he **wailed**, "I lost my GameMaster a little while ago. I should have been more careful!"

Afterward, Mom and I walked home. I was glad I **returned** the toy to the boy. So, I made a promise to myself to always try to do the right thing. Now that is a vow I can keep!

Daniel Griffo

Make Connections

? How are Paul and Wyatt good citizens? ESSENTIAL QUESTION

What is something you do to be a good citizen? TEXT TO SELF

Text Evidence

1 Comprehension
Point of View

Reread the first paragraph. Underline how Wyatt describes the boy who lost the toy.

2 Specific Vocabulary Ⓐ Ⓒ Ⓣ

When you *return* something, you give it back to its owner. Box how Wyatt feels after he returned the toy to the boy.

COLLABORATE

3 Talk About It

Discuss how Wyatt acts like a good citizen. What does he promise to do always?

_____

_____

_____.

Respond to the Text

Partner Discussion Answer the questions. Discuss what you learned about "A Difficult Decision." Write the page numbers where you found text evidence.

What happens when Wyatt finds the game?

At first, Wyatt believes _____.

Paul tells Wyatt that _____.

Wyatt decides _____ because _____.

Text Evidence 🔍

Page(s): _____

Page(s): _____

Page(s): _____

How do Paul and Wyatt act like good citizens?

Paul is happy that Wyatt _____.

Paul and Wyatt walk around _____.

After returning the game, Wyatt _____.

Text Evidence 🔍

Page(s): _____

Page(s): _____

Page(s): _____

Group Discussion Present your answers to the group. Cite text evidence to justify your thinking. Listen to and discuss the group's opinions about your answers.

COLLABORATE

Write Review your notes. Then write your answer to the Essential Question. Use text evidence to support your answer. Use vocabulary words in your writing.

> **Why are Wyatt and Paul good citizens?**
>
> Paul tells Wyatt _____
>
> _____.
>
> At school, Wyatt helps _____
>
> _____.
>
> Wyatt and Paul _____
>
> _____.
>
> _____

COLLABORATE

Share Writing Present your writing to the class. Discuss their opinions. Think about what the class has to say. Do they justify their claims? Explain why you agree or disagree.

I agree with _____ because _____.

I disagree because _____.

Jordan

Take Notes About the Text I took notes to respond to the prompt: *Do you think Wyatt should give back the GameMaster? Give reasons to support your claim.*

pages 290–293

Wyatt finds and claims the lost toy.

Paul says that it is wrong to keep it.

Wyatt's Decision

A boy bursts into tears when he sees his game.

Wyatt gives advice to other kids, and he knows the right thing to do.

Write About the Text I used my notes from my idea map to write my opinion about Wyatt's decision.

Student Model: *Opinion*

I think Wyatt should not keep the GameMaster. It does not belong to him. I agree with Paul. It is wrong to keep it. Wyatt gives kids advice at school. He knows that he should give the game back. Wyatt also knows the owner will be upset to lose it. Wyatt is a good citizen to give the toy back.

TALK ABOUT IT

Text Evidence **Box** a detail from the web in Jordan's paragraph. Does this detail support the opinion?

Grammar **Circle** the third sentence. How can you add *strongly* to the sentence?

Connect Ideas **Underline** the first two sentences. How can you combine the sentences with the word *because*?

Your Turn

Do you think Paul is a good friend to Wyatt? Give reasons in your answer.

>> *Go Digital*
Write your response online. Use your editing checklist.

297

COLLABORATE

How do the kids cooperate? What are some things you do when you cooperate with others? Write your ideas on the web.

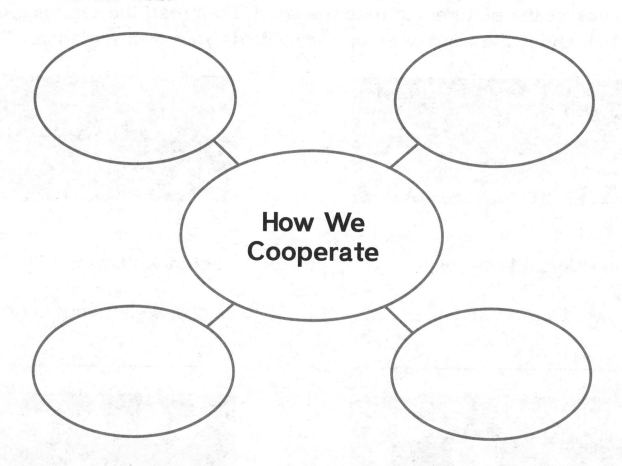

How We Cooperate

Discuss what you do when you cooperate with others. Use the words from the web. You can say:

When I cooperate, I _____, _____,

and _____.

More Vocabulary

COLLABORATE

Look at the picture and read the word. Then read the sentence. Talk about the word with a partner. Write your own sentence.

blocked

The goalie **blocked** the goal.

Another word for *blocked* is _____

_____.

calm

The water is **calm** and still.

The water is *calm* when _____

_____.

chat

I **chat** with my friends.

I *chat* with friends during _____

_____.

disappointing

It was **disappointing** when our team lost.

_____ was *disappointing*

because _____.

greeted

My teacher **greeted** me this morning.

I *greeted* _____

by _____.

reported

We **reported** about our day at dinner.

Another word for *reported* is _____

_____.

Words and Phrases
Adverbs *just*

just = very much
Caroline <u>just</u> loves to dance.

just = only
There is <u>just</u> one apple left.

just = a short time ago

We just moved here.

Read each sentence. Circle the meaning of the underlined word.

We <u>just</u> started school last week.

very much   a short time ago

I have <u>just</u> one red shirt.

only   very much

We <u>just</u> love to watch the dogs play.

a short time ago   very much

» Go Digital **Add the adverb *just* to your New Words notebook. Write a sentence to show each meaning.**

(t)Hero Images/Getty Images; (b)Ariel Skelley/Blend Images/Getty Images

❶ Talk About It

Look at the picture. Read the title. Talk about what you see. Write your ideas.

What does the title tell you?

_____

_____

_____.

What are the characters doing?

_____

_____.

Take notes as you read the story.

SOCCER FRIENDS

Essential Question

How do people get along?

Read about a girl who learns to get along with others on the soccer field.

Kelly couldn't wait until soccer season began. She could not be patient because she just loved racing to get the ball. She would use her imagination to picture the ball, and then she would fly toward it. Kelly practiced at home during the **calm**, peaceful mornings.

At the first team practice, Kelly **greeted** her friends. She liked to **chat** and interact with them. Then she saw a new girl. "That's Selena. She's a really fast runner," **reported** Kelly's friend Tara.

At first, Kelly held her tongue and said nothing. She was **worried**. She had always been the fastest runner on the team. Then she said, "I can beat her."

When practice started, Coach Troy had everyone line up for races. Kelly was nervous and had butterflies in her stomach.

Richard Johnson

❶ **Comprehension**
Point of View

How does Kelly feel about playing soccer? Support your answer with details from the first paragraph.

_____

_____

_____.

❷ **Specific Vocabulary** Ⓐ Ⓒ Ⓣ

When you are *worried*, you feel nervous. Why is Kelly worried about a fast runner on her team? Box the answer.

❸ **Sentence Structure** Ⓐ Ⓒ Ⓣ

Reread the first sentence in the last paragraph. A comma separates two parts of the sentence. Circle the part that tells what happens when practice starts.

303

1 Specific Vocabulary ACT

The verb *to match* can mean "to be as good as someone else." When is Kelly not as good as Selena?

Kelly cannot match Selena

_____

2 Sentence Structure ACT

Reread the second paragraph. Box the word that connects two parts of the second sentence. Circle the part that tells you Kelly does not laugh with the girls.

3 Comprehension
Point of View

Reread the fourth paragraph. Box the sentence that shows how Kelly feels about losing the races.

"On your mark, get set, GO!" the coach shouted. Kelly ran as fast as she could but she noticed Selena getting ahead of her. Kelly tried her best but couldn't **match** Selena.

Later, Kelly watched as Selena entertained some girls by bouncing the ball on her head. The girls laughed, but Kelly was not amused.

That night, Mom could tell Kelly was upset. "Can you describe what's wrong?" she asked.

"A new girl named Selena beat me at the races. It stinks to get beaten!" said Kelly.

"I know that's **disappointing** for you," Mom said. "But it also sounds like good news for your team." Kelly thought about her Mom's words. She cared about the team, but she liked being the fastest.

At the next practice, the team played a game. Kelly and Selena were on the same team and Selena was goalie. She quickly **blocked** a goal.

Then Kelly got the ball and **thumped** it hard toward the net. She scored the winning goal!

After practice, Selena said to Kelly, "You were really great today."

"Thanks, so were you. I think our team can be great if we cooperate and work together," said Kelly.

"I think you're right about that," said Selena.

"I'd love to keep playing," Kelly said. "Want to come over to my house and practice?"

Make Connections

? How does Kelly learn to get along with Selena on the soccer field? ESSENTIAL QUESTION

Compare Kelly's problem to a time you have had to work to get along with others. TEXT TO SELF

Text Evidence

1 Specific Vocabulary ⓐⒸⓉ

The word *thumped* means "kicked or hit." Underline what happens when Kelly thumped the ball.

2 Comprehension
Point of View

Reread the fourth paragraph. Circle the reason Kelly thinks the team can be great.

COLLABORATE

3 Talk About It

Discuss how Kelly feels about Selena at the end of the story. What does Kelly invite Selena to do?

_____

_____

_____

Respond to the Text

Partner Discussion Answer the questions. Discuss what you learned about "Soccer Friends." Write the page numbers where you found text evidence.

How does Kelly feel when the story begins?	**Text Evidence**
Kelly is excited for _____.	Page(s): _____
She is worried because _____.	Page(s): _____
Selena wins the race, and Kelly _____.	Page(s): _____

What events lead Kelly to get along with Selena?	**Text Evidence**
At the next practice, _____.	Page(s): _____
Kelly tells Selena that their team _____.	Page(s): _____
Kelly invites Selena _____.	Page(s): _____

Group Discussion Present your answers to the group. Cite text evidence to justify your thinking. Listen to and discuss the group's opinions about your answers.

Write Review your notes. Then write your answer to the Essential Question. Use text evidence to support your answer. Use vocabulary words in your writing.

COLLABORATE

How does Kelly learn to get along with Selena?

Kelly's mom tells her _____

_____.

At the next practice, _____

_____.

Kelly learns that she and Selena _____

_____.

Share Writing Present your writing to the class. Discuss their opinions. Think about what the class has to say. Do they justify their claims? Explain why you agree or disagree.

COLLABORATE

I agree with _____ because _____.

I disagree because _____.

Write to Sources

pages 302–305

Take Notes About the Text I took notes to respond to the prompt: *Do you think Kelly should be friends with Selena? Write your opinion.*

Rachel

First, Kelly wants to beat Selena but Selena is faster.

↓

Then Kelly's mom tells her that Selena is good news for the team.

↓

At practice, Selena blocked a goal and Kelly scored the winning goal.

↓

Finally, Kelly says that the team will be great if she and Selena work together.

308

Write About the Text I used my notes from my chart to write my opinion.

Student Model: *Opinion*

I think Kelly should be friends with Selena. At first, Kelly is upset that she lost to Selena. Kelly's mom tells Kelly that Selena can help the team. At the next practice, Kelly plays well. Selena plays well, too. Kelly understands that the team will be great if they work together. Kelly should be Selena's friend so they can have fun playing soccer together!

TALK ABOUT IT

COLLABORATE

Text Evidence **Underline** the sentence that tells what Kelly understands. How does this detail support Rachel's claim?

Grammar **Box** the third sentence. What pronoun can replace the name *Kelly* in this sentence?

Condense Ideas **Circle** the sentences that tell how the girls played at practice. How can you combine the sentences?

Your Turn

COLLABORATE

Would you want Selena on your soccer team? Give reasons from the text to support your opinion.

>> Go Digital
Write your response online. Use your editing checklist.

TALK ABOUT IT

Weekly Concept Our Heroes

? **Essential Question**
What do heroes do?

>> *Go Digital*

U.S. COAST GUARD   AIRRANGER

310

COLLABORATE What does a rescue worker do that makes him or her a hero? Who are some heroes that you know? What makes someone a hero? Write your ideas on the chart.

Hero	What Makes Them a Hero

Discuss people that you think are heroes. Tell what they do that makes them heroes. Use the words from the chart. You can say:

_____ are heroes because

_____.

More Vocabulary

 Look at the picture and read the word. Then read the sentence.
Talk about the word with a partner. Write your own sentence.

afford

Karen can **afford** to buy a gift.

To *afford* a gift means _____

_____.

brave

Firefighters are **brave**.

Firefighters are *brave* because _____

_____.

improve

I practice to **improve** my playing.

I want to *improve* _____

_____.

punished

Dan **punished** his dog.

People get *punished* for _____

_____.

312

respect

We show **respect** for the flag.

I show *respect* for adults when _____

_____.

struggles

The snow caused **struggles** for many.

Another word for *struggles* is _____

_____.

The words *there* and *their* sound the same. The two words have different spellings and meanings.

<u>There</u> are apples in the bowl.

The children read <u>their</u> books.

Write *there* or *their* to complete each sentence.

_____ are three dogs in the yard.

There   Their

The horses ate _____ food.

                        there   their

» *Go Digital* Add the words *there* and *their* to your New Words notebook. Write a sentence to show the meaning of each word.

COLLABORATE

1 Talk About It

Look at the picture. Read the title. Talk about what you see. Write your ideas.

What does the title tell you?

_____

_____

_____.

What do the pictures show?

_____

_____

_____

_____.

Take notes as you read the text.

César Chávez

Essential Question

?

What do heroes do?

Read about a man who took action to improve the lives of others.

Who are your heroes? For many farm workers, César Chávez is a hero. He is the **brave** man who spent his life helping them.

Childhood

César Chávez was born in Arizona. His parents taught him about learning, hard work, and **respect**.

César worked on the family farm as a young boy. He helped care for the farm animals. His mother and grandmother taught César about caring. Many people came to their door asking for food, and his kind family always shared.

César had a strong interest in education. This **desire** to learn was sometimes hard on him. Spanish was his first language, but he needed to learn and study English. At school, he was **punished** for speaking Spanish.

His mother taught César to find peaceful ways to solve problems. These lessons helped him succeed later in life. He would win **struggles** without fighting.

Margaret Lindmark

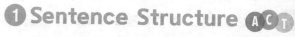

Text Evidence

1 Sentence Structure Ⓐ🄲🅃

Reread the second sentence in the section titled "Childhood." Commas separate three things César's parents taught him. Circle each of these things.

2 Comprehension

Sequence

Reread the third paragraph. Circle what César did on the family farm as a young boy.

3 Specific Vocabulary Ⓐ🄲🅃

Reread the fourth paragraph. To have a *desire* to learn means to want to learn. Why was this desire sometimes hard for César? Underline details that explain why.

Text Evidence

1 Specific Vocabulary Ⓐ Ⓒ Ⓣ

Underline the words that tell the meaning of *drought*. What happened when the drought caused the farm's

crops to die? _____

_____

_____

2 Comprehension
Sequence

Reread the first sentence in the second paragraph. Box where the family then moved. On the timeline, box the year this happened.

COLLABORATE

3 Talk About It

Discuss why migrant farm workers had difficult lives. Circle what happened if workers complained?

316

Hard Times

When César was ten, it did not rain for a long time. This **drought** caused the plants on the farm to die. Without crops to sell, César's family couldn't **afford** to keep the farm.

Then César's family moved to California where there was no drought. His family traveled from farm to farm and worked the crops.

César and his family would quickly discover that migrant farm workers had difficult lives. Their challenging jobs forced them to work long hours for little money. The workers bent over all day tending the crops. The work they had to perform made their backs hurt and their fingers bleed. If workers complained, farm owners fired them.

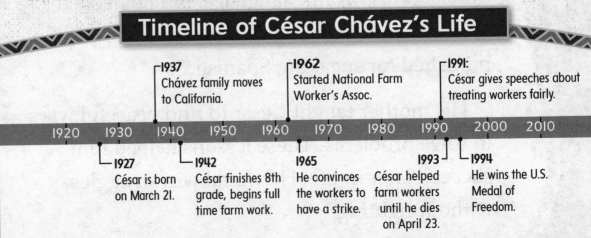

Timeline of César Chávez's Life

1937 Chávez family moves to California.

1962 Started National Farm Worker's Assoc.

1991: César gives speeches about treating workers fairly.

1920   1930   1940   1950   1960   1970   1980   1990   2000   2010

1927 César is born on March 21.

1942 César finishes 8th grade, begins full time farm work.

1965 He convinces the workers to have a strike.

1993 César helped farm workers until he dies on April 23.

1994 He wins the U.S. Medal of Freedom.

Changing Lives

César knew the migrant workers were not treated fairly so he decided to take action. He told the migrant workers he had a plan.

It was time for grapes to be harvested, or picked. César told the workers to stop working. This was called a strike. The grapes began to rot. With no grapes to sell, the landowners lost money. Finally, the owners talked to César. They promised better pay. After that, the workers began picking the crops again.

César Chávez worked for the rest of his life to **improve** farm workers' lives. Would you agree that he is a hero?

Make Connections

? How do César Chávez's actions make him a hero? ESSENTIAL QUESTION

How have you ever tried to help others? TEXT TO SELF

Margaret Lindmark

1 Sentence Structure Ⓐ Ⓒ Ⓣ

The word *so* connects two parts of the first sentence. Circle the part that tells why César decided to take action.

2 Comprehension
Sequence

Reread the second paragraph. Underline what landowners did after they lost money. Box what happened after that.

COLLABORATE

3 Talk About It

Discuss how César helped workers get better pay. Look back at the timeline. How did César help workers in 1991?

_____

_____

_____ .

317

Respond to the Text

Partner Discussion Answer the questions. Discuss what you learned about "César Chávez." Write the page numbers where you found text evidence.

What did César Chávez learn about in childhood?

Text Evidence

César's family taught him _____.   Page(s): _____

He learned to find peaceful _____.   Page(s): _____

In California, César learned _____.   Page(s): _____

Describe how César helped farm workers.

Text Evidence

César told the farm workers to _____.   Page(s): _____

Landowners talked to César and _____.   Page(s): _____

César continued to help _____.   Page(s): _____

Group Discussion Present your answers to the group. Cite text evidence to justify your thinking. Listen to and discuss the group's opinions about your answers.

Write Review your notes. Then write your answer to the Essential Question. Use text evidence to support your answer. Use vocabulary words in your writing.

What made César Chávez a hero?

As a boy, César _____.

César learned that farm workers were _____

_____.

If farm workers complained, _____.

César helped farm workers _____.

As a result, landowners _____.

César gave speeches _____.

Share Writing Present your writing to the class. Discuss their opinions. Think about what the class has to say. Do they justify their claims? Explain why you agree or disagree.

I agree with _____ because _____. I disagree because _____.

Write to Sources

pages 314–317

Take Notes About the Text I took notes about the text on this chart to respond to the prompt: *How did a drought change César's life? Write the sequence of events.*

Ahmed

The drought caused the family to lose the farm.

↓

They moved to California and became migrant farm workers.

↓

César learned that farm workers were not treated fairly.

↓

César worked the rest of his life to improve farm workers' lives.

Write About the Text I used my notes to describe how a drought changed César's life.

When César was ten, a drought changed César's life. The family lost their farm. César's family moved to California. In California, they traveled from farm to farm. They were farm workers. They worked hard for little money. César decided to work to improve the lives of the farm workers. He became a hero.

TALK ABOUT IT

Text Evidence **Underline** the sentence that tells how farm workers were treated unfairly. Why is this a supporting detail?

Grammar **Circle** the words "César's life" in the first sentence. What possessive pronoun can replace the word *César's*?

Condense Ideas **Box** the third and fourth sentences. How can you combine the sentences?

Your Turn

Tell about important events in César Chávez's life in order. Use text evidence to support your answer.

>> *Go Digital*
Write your response online. Use your editing checklist.

321

TALK ABOUT IT

Weekly Concept Preserving Our Earth

? **Essential Question**
How can we protect the Earth?

>> *Go Digital*

322

COLLABORATE

How are the kids protecting the Earth? What do you do that helps preserve, or protect, the Earth's resources? Write your ideas on the web.

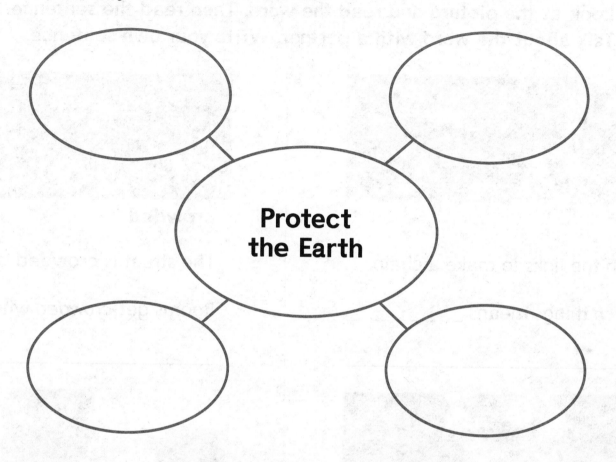

Protect
the Earth

Describe some things you do to protect the Earth. Use the words from the web. You can say:

I protect the Earth when I _____

_____.

Yi Lu/Corbis

More Vocabulary

 Look at the picture and read the word. Then read the sentence.
Talk about the word with a partner. Write your own sentence.

attach

I **attach** the links to make a chain.

To *attach* things means _____

_____.

creative

The children are **creative**.

I am *creative* when _____

_____.

crowded

The street is **crowded** with people.

Rooms get *crowded* when _____

_____.

accepted

The children gladly **accepted** the award.

People accept _____

that others give them.

324

materials

Crayons and paints are art **materials**.

My favorite art *materials* are _____

_____ .

suggested

We **suggested** names for our pet.

At recess, I *suggested* that_____

_____ .

Words and Phrases
Adjectives *another* and *each*

another = one more of the same thing
I read <u>*another*</u> book about horses.

each = all the things in a group
We cleaned <u>each</u> desk in our class.

Write *another* or *each* to complete the sentences.

Sheila is_____ student in my class.

_____ student in the class works

with a partner.

>> *Go Digital* **Add the words *another* and *each* to your New Words notebook. Write a sentence to show the meaning of each word.**

COLLABORATE

1 Talk About It

Look at the picture. Read the title. Talk about what you see. Write your ideas.

What does the title tell you?

_____

_____

_____.

What is the class doing?

_____

_____

_____

Take notes as you read the story.

The Art Project

Art Contest

Essential Question

? How can we protect the Earth?

Read about how a class saves Earth's resources.

"Look! The community center is having an art contest," said Grace. She was holding a **flyer**.

Mrs. Simon read the flyer aloud. Everyone agreed they would like to enter the art contest. Mrs. Simon said, "Our classroom supply of art **materials** is low because it's the end of the year. I'll check with Mrs. Rice to see what she has."

Mrs. Rice, the art teacher, didn't have any art materials. "I won't be getting a supply until next year," she said. The whole class was disappointed. "How can we enter the art contest without art materials?" asked Grace.

"Maybe we can raise some money. We could have a bake sale," **suggested** Hal.

"I don't think there's time," Mrs. Simon said.

"Let's use the paper in the recycling bin," Pablo said. Pablo did not often raise his hand. He rarely spoke up, so everyone was surprised when he offered an idea.

Kristen Sorra

❶ Specific Vocabulary **A**C**T**

Reread the first paragraph. A *flyer* is a piece of paper that tells about a special event. Circle the special event.

❷ Sentence Structure **A**C**T**

Reread the first sentence in the third paragraph. Box the commas. Circle the words that tell who Mrs. Rice is.

❸ Comprehension
Problem and Solution

Reread the third paragraph. Why can't the class enter the art contest?

_____

_____.

Reread the rest of the page. Underline what Pablo suggests to solve this problem.

327

Text Evidence

1 Comprehension
Problem and Solution

Reread the second paragraph. Pablo explains why recycled paper saves Earth's resources. Underline the reason why.

2 Specific Vocabulary A**C**T

Find the word *fold*. If you fold paper, you bend it. Pablo says the class can fold the paper into a shape of a bird. Circle the type of bird.

COLLABORATE

3 Talk About It

Explain how the kids make the mobile for the art contest.

_____

_____

_____

Hal said, "I'm curious about your idea. I want to learn why you would use old paper."

"So we can save Earth's resources," replied Pablo. "When we use recycled paper, we use natural materials and save trees."

"We can also use this old string and these wire hangers," added Grace.

Now the class had to decide what to do with the materials. Pablo had another idea. "We can **fold** the paper into cranes. Then we can **attach** the cranes to a frame to make a mobile."

Mrs. Simon taught the children how to fold the paper into cranes. Then everyone helped attach the cranes to the mobile.

On the day of the art contest, the paper crane mobile hung in the enormous community center room. The huge space was **crowded** with art projects. From far off, the class spotted their project. The crane mobile swayed gently as people walked past. From a distance, the paper cranes appeared to be softly flying.

The judges checked each art project. They looked closely at the crane mobile.

The paper crane mobile won the prize for the most **creative** use of materials. As the class proudly **accepted** their prize, they could not stop grinning. Grace exclaimed, "We made our art project, and we saved the Earth at the same time!"

Make Connections

? What do the children do at school to help protect the Earth? ESSENTIAL QUESTION

Tell about a way you can help protect Earth's resources at school. TEXT TO SELF

Text Evidence

1 Sentence Structure Ⓐ Ⓒ Ⓣ

Reread the first sentence. Underline where the paper crane mobile hangs on the day of the art contest.

COLLABORATE

2 Talk About It

Talk about what happens as people walk past the mobile. From a distance, what do the cranes appear to be doing?

_____

_____

_____.

3 Comprehension
Problem and Solution

Reread the last paragraph. Circle the prize the art project wins. Underline what the kids save at the same time.

329

Respond to the Text

Partner Discussion Answer the questions. Discuss what you learned about "The Art Project." Write the page numbers where you found text evidence.

Why does Pablo speak up in class?

Text Evidence 🔍

The Community Center is having _____.

Page(s): _____

It is the end of the year, and _____.

Page(s): _____

Pablo suggests _____.

Page(s): _____

How does the class help save Earth's resources?

Text Evidence 🔍

Pablo tells the class that using _____.

Page(s): _____

Grace suggests that they _____.

Page(s): _____

The art project wins a prize _____.

Page(s): _____

Group Discussion Present your answers to the group. Cite text evidence to justify your thinking. Listen to and discuss the group's opinions about your answers.

Write Review your notes. Then write your answer to the Essential Question. Use text evidence to support your answer. Use vocabulary words in your writing.

How do the children help protect the Earth?

The children want to enter _____

but _____.

Pablo suggests that they can _____

_____.

Pablo explains this will _____.

The children make _____.

They win a prize for_____.

Share Writing Present your writing to the class. Discuss their opinions. Think about what the class has to say. Do they justify their claims? Explain why you agree or disagree.

I agree with _____ because _____. I disagree because _____.

Write to Sources

pages 326–329

Take Notes About the Text I took notes to respond to the prompt: *Grace and Pablo talk about winning the prize. Write a dialogue about what they say.*

Hannah

Grace's Words	Pablo's Words
How can the class enter the art contest without art materials?	The class can use paper in the recycling bin for the art project.
The class can also use old string and wire hangers.	"When we use recycled paper, we use natural materials and save trees."
"We made our art project, and we saved the Earth at the same time!"	The class can fold the paper into cranes, and attach the cranes to a frame to make a mobile.

Write About the Text I added a dialogue between Grace and Pablo to the story.

Student Model: *Narrative Text*

Grace said, "Pablo earned the prize. His ideas won the prize."

"I am glad you had the idea to use the string and wire hangers," Pablo said. "We are a good team."

"I'm proud," Grace said. "We used old materials in a very creative way."

Pablo said, "This prize goes to the whole class. We all worked together to earn it!"

TALK ABOUT IT

Text Evidence **Box** the first and second sentences. Why does Grace think Pablo's ideas won the prize?

Grammar **Circle** the sentence Pablo says about the class being a good team. How can you write "we are" as a contraction?

Connect Ideas **Underline** the last two sentences. How can you combine them using the word *because*?

Your Turn

Think about what Pablo tells his mom about winning. Write a dialogue that tells what they say.

>> *Go Digital*
Write your response online. Use your editing checklist.

333

TALK ABOUT IT

Weekly Concept Rights and Rules

? Essential Question
Why are rules important?

>> *Go Digital*

334

COLLABORATE What rules are the kids following? What rules do you follow? Why are the rules important? Write your ideas on the chart.

Rule	Why It Is Important

Discuss the rules that you follow and why they are important. Use the words from the chart. You can say:

Some rules that I follow are _____

_____. These rules are important because _____

_____.

More Vocabulary

Look at the picture and read the word. Then read the sentence.
Talk about the word with a partner. Write your own sentence.

announce

Sarah will **announce** the winners.

Teachers *announce* _____

_____ to students.

elected

I hope to get **elected** class president.

I know _____ was

elected to be _____.

explored

The children **explored** the museum.

I *explored* _____

_____.

order

The teacher keeps **order** in the room.

Order is important because _____

_____.

(tl)Fancy/SuperStock; (tr)Bananastock/age fotostock; (bl)Steve Debenport/E+/Getty Images; (br)Wealan Pollard/age fotostock

336

recently

It **recently** snowed.

I *recently* _____

_____ .

statement

The mayor just gave a **statement**.

A *statement* is something important

you _____ or _____ .

free from = **do not have anymore**
Last week, I had a cold. But now I am <u>free from</u> feeling sick.

took place = **happened**
The picnic <u>took place</u> in the park.

Read the sentences below. Write *took place* or *free from* to complete the sentences.

In summer, we are _____ cold weather.

The race _____ last week.

>> *Go Digital* **Add the phrases *free from* and *took place* to your New Words notebook. Write a sentence to show the meaning of each phrase.**

COLLABORATE

❶ Talk About It

Look at the photos. Read the title. Talk about what you see. Write your ideas.

What does the title tell you?

_____

_____

_____.

What do the photos show?

_____

_____

_____.

Take notes as you read the text.

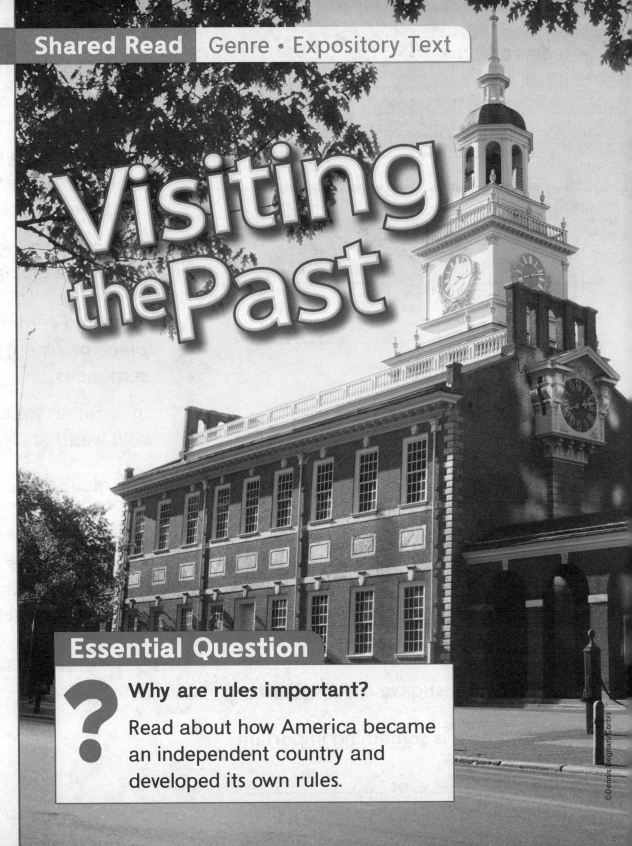

Visiting the Past

Essential Question

?

Why are rules important?

Read about how America became an independent country and developed its own rules.

©Dennis Degnan/Corbis

On the Fourth of July, skies across the United States light up. It's Independence Day! The holiday celebrates the Declaration of Independence.

The Changs visit Philadelphia.

In 1776, this **statement** was written to tell the King of England that the colonies were free from his rule. The colonies would be united to form a new country together.

Janet Chang, 8, **recently** visited Philadelphia with her family. Philadelphia was the first capital of the United States. The Changs went there to learn about their country's history or past.

Busy Building

First, they went to Independence Hall. "That's where the Declaration of Independence was **signed**," Janet exclaimed. She was excited to be there.

MIXA/Getty Images

Text Evidence

1 Sentence Structure A C T

Reread the first paragraph. Circle the contraction *it's*. What date is Independence Day on?

It's on _____

_____.

2 Comprehension
Cause and Effect

Reread the second paragraph. Circle what the Declaration of Independence told the King of England. Box what happened as a result of this.

3 Specific Vocabulary A C T

Find the word *signed*. When people sign a statement, they agree to what it says. Where was the Declaration of Independence signed?

_____

339

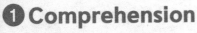

Text Evidence

① Comprehension
Cause and Effect

Reread the first paragraph. What is the effect of having rules? Underline the sentence that tells you.

② Specific Vocabulary ACT

Find the word *state*. In the text, *state* means "to make a statement, or to say something important." What are people allowed to state because of the Constitution?

Americans can state _____

_____.

COLLABORATE

③ Talk About It

Talk about what the Liberty Bell announced in the past. What did the bell announce on July 8, 1776?

The signers of the Declaration of Independence.

Ten years after the Declaration of Independence, the Constitution was written in Independence Hall. The writers of the Constitution created new rules for the country. Rules are important. They help to keep **order** in a country and give people rights. One new rule was that people could **state** their opinion.

Ringing for Freedom

The Changs later visited the Liberty Bell. It is said that the famous bell rang on July 8, 1776. That's when the first public reading of the Declaration of Independence took place. The bell also chimed to **announce** important events, such as when a President was **elected**.

Visit Philadelphia!

Famous Place	Why It Is Cool
The National Constitution Center	It explains the rules that were created for our nation. One area tells of the right to say what you want and the right to vote.
Independence Hall	This is where the Declaration of Independence and the Constitution were written. You can see the chair that George Washington sat in as he signed the Constitution.
Betsy Ross House	It is said that Betsy Ross made the first American flag. You can tour her home to see how she lived and worked.

Memorable Moments

Finally, Janet and her family **explored** Franklin Court. This is where Benjamin Franklin lived and worked. Franklin was one of the writers of the Declaration of Independence. He also helped frame the Constitution.

To remember their visit, the Changs mailed a postcard from Franklin's post office. "I'll never forget this day!" Janet said.

Make Connections

? What is one rule of our country? Why are rules important? ESSENTIAL QUESTION

How is this rule the same or different from your rules at school? TEXT TO SELF

(t) Wadsworth Atheneum Museum of Art / Art Resource, NY; (b) Tetra Images/Alamy

Text Evidence

1 Sentence Structure A C T

Read the first two sentences. The second sentence describes a place. Circle the name of the place. Box what Benjamin Franklin did there.

2 Comprehension
Cause and Effect

What is an effect of the family visit to Philadelphia? Circle the text that shows how Janet feels at the end of the trip.

COLLABORATE

3 Talk About It

Discuss the famous places in the chart. What can you see at the Betsy Ross House?

_____

_____

Respond to the Text

Partner Discussion Answer the questions. Discuss what you learned about "Visiting the Past." Write the page numbers where you found text evidence.

What important places did Janet learn about?

Independence Hall was where _____.

The Liberty Bell _____.

Franklin Court was where _____.

Text Evidence 🔍

Page(s): _____

Page(s): _____

Page(s): _____

What did Janet learn about the Constitution?

The writers of the Constitution created _____.

These rules are important because _____.

One new rule was _____.

Text Evidence 🔍

Page(s): _____

Page(s): _____

Page(s): _____

Group Discussion Present your answers to the group. Cite text evidence to justify your thinking. Listen to and discuss the group's opinions about your answers.

Write Review your notes. Then write your answer to the Essential Question. Use text evidence to support your answer. Use vocabulary words in your writing.

What did Janet learn about her country and its rules?

Independence Hall was where _____

_____.

The Liberty Bell rang when _____

_____.

The Constitution created _____ to help

_____.

One new rule is _____.

Share Writing Present your writing to the class. Discuss their opinions. Think about what the class has to say. Do they justify their claims? Explain why you agree or disagree. You can say:

I agree with _____ because _____. I disagree because _____.

Write to Sources

pages 338–341

Take Notes About the Text I took notes on an idea web to respond to the prompt: *What was the author's purpose for writing "Visiting the Past"? Use text evidence in your answer.*

Dean

The Declaration of Independence was signed in Independence Hall.

The Constitution was written in Independence Hall.

The Changs visit Philadelphia and learn about our history.

Liberty Bell rang for important events.

Benjamin Franklin helped write the Declaration of Independence.

344

Write About the Text I used my notes to explain why the author wrote the text.

Student Model: *Informative Text*

The author tells about important places that are in Philadelphia. Janet Chang learned that the Declaration of Independence and Constitution were signed in Independence Hall. She learned how our country became independent. She also learned about Ben Franklin. The Changs explored Franklin Court. The author explains why Philadelphia is an important place in American history.

TALK ABOUT IT

Text Evidence Underline what Janet learned at Independece Hall. How do these details support Dean's paragraph?

Grammar Circle the first sentence. How can you add the phrase *in American history* to the sentence?

Connect Ideas Box the fourth and fifth sentences. How can you use the word *when* to connect the ideas?

Your Turn

Write a paragraph about the family's visit to the Liberty Bell. Include details from the text.

>> *Go Digital*
Write your response online. Use your editing checklist.

How on Earth?

The Big Idea

What keeps our world working?

Weekly Concept Plant Myths and Facts

Essential Question
What do myths help us understand?

>> *Go Digital*

COLLABORATE

Describe the plants you see. What is the myth about the plants called bluebells? What other myths about plants do you know? Write your ideas on the web.

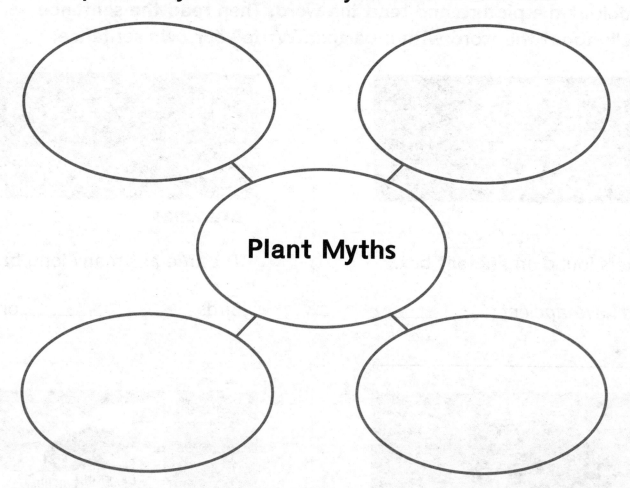

Plant Myths

Discuss myths about plants. What do the myths explain or tell about? Use the words from the web. You can say:

I know a myth about _____.

This myth explains _____.

More Vocabulary

COLLABORATE

Look at the picture and read the word. Then read the sentence. Talk about the word with a partner. Write your own sentence.

ancient

The workers found an **ancient** box.

Museums have *ancient* _____

_____.

approached

Lisa **approached** her friend to talk.

I *approached* a friend to _____

_____.

branches

The tree has many long **branches**.

Birds _____ on *branches*.

breeze

The flag is waving in the **breeze**.

Another word for *breeze* is _____.

350

purpose

An umbrella's **purpose** is to keep you dry.

Another word for *purpose* is _____.

reasons

Being fit is a good **reason** to exercise.

The *reason* I like _____ is

_____.

Words and Phrases

Homophones *friends'* and *friends*

friends' = belonging to friends
I play at my <u>friends'</u> houses.

friends = more than one friend
I like to go to the park with my <u>friends</u>.

Read the sentences below. Write *friends'* or *friends* to complete each sentence.

My _____ toys are fun to play with.

Jaime has three _____ who live on her street.

>> Go Digital **Add the words *friends'* and *friends* to your New Words notebook. Write a sentence to show the meaning of each word.**

COLLABORATE

1 Talk About It

Look at the picture. Read the title. Talk about what you see. Write your ideas.

What does the title tell you?

_____

_____

_____ .

What does the picture tell you about the four trees?

_____

_____

_____ .

Take notes as you read the story.

Why Fir Tree Keeps His Leaves

Essential Question

? **What do myths help us understand?**

Read about a tree that learns why he does not develop like other trees.

Long ago, in **ancient** times, Mother Nature gave each tree a different **purpose**. However, she did not share her **reasons** with the trees.

Fir Tree had three friends—Maple, Oak, and Elm. During the first summer, they saw Bird and Squirrel play in Farmer's corn and tomato crops. The **breeze** blew and rustled their leaves. The shining sun warmed them.

Then the first fall arrived. Farmer harvested what he had grown. Maple, Oak, and Elm's leaves turned beautiful shades of orange, red, and yellow. The leaves shone as golden as the Sun. Fir Tree's leaves stayed green.

Fir Tree complained to Mother Nature, "I don't like my leaves. I want them to change colors like my friends' leaves."

"Be patient," Mother Nature replied. "You will learn your purpose."

Xiao Xin

Text Evidence

① Comprehension

Theme

Reread the first paragraph. Underline the sentence that tells how Fir Tree is different from his friends.

② Specific Vocabulary Ⓐ Ⓒ Ⓣ

Reread the second paragraph. The phrase *period of life* tells about a time in your life. Why is Fir Tree stuck in one period of his life?

Fir tree doesn't have stages

_____

_____ .

③ Sentence Structure Ⓐ Ⓒ Ⓣ

Read the last paragraph. Circle the character that the pronoun *she* refers to. Box what she asks Maple to build.

So Fir Tree waited. The temperature dropped even more. Bird flew south, and Squirrel was nowhere around. Maple, Oak, and Elm lost their leaves, but Fir Tree's green leaves remained. Soon snow blanketed the ground.

Again, Fir Tree protested to Mother Nature. "Why am I different? Why don't I have stages and change like my friends? I seem to be stuck in one **period of life**!"

"Be patient," Mother Nature replied. "Soon you will develop an understanding of your purpose."

Just then, Squirrel appeared on the edge of the forest. She was cold. When she went inside the forest, she saw Maple. She asked if she could build a warm nest in his **branches**.

Maple said he didn't have any leaves. She asked Oak and then Elm. Both said the same thing as Maple. She was still **bitterly** cold.

Squirrel **approached** Fir Tree. "Excuse me," she said. "May I build a nest in your branches?"

"Yes, that would be nice," said Fir Tree. Squirrel ran up Fir Tree's branches, and she made her nest. Soon, she was warm, comfortable, and asleep.

Fir Tree finally understood that his green leaves provided a warm shelter for animals in the winter. From that moment on, Fir Tree was happy to be different. Still today, he remains proud of his evergreen leaves.

Make Connections

? How did Fir Tree develop differently from his friends? ESSENTIAL QUESTION

When have you wanted to be like your friends? TEXT TO SELF

Xiao Xin

Text Evidence

1 Specific Vocabulary ACT

The word *bitterly* can mean "very badly." Circle how Squirrel feels with no nest.

2 Sentence Structure ACT

Reread the last sentence in the third paragraph. Circle the adjectives that describe Squirrel in her nest.

3 Comprehension
Theme

Reread the last paragraph. What is the purpose of Fir Tree's green leaves?

_____

_____

_____.

Underline how Fir Tree feels when he understands the purpose of his green leaves.

Respond to the Text

Partner Discussion Answer the questions. Discuss what you
learned about "Why Fir Tree Keeps His Leaves." Write the
page numbers where you found text evidence.

How is Fir Tree different from other trees?

Text Evidence 🔍

Fir Tree's leaves do not change _____.   Page(s): _____

In winter, Fir Tree's friends _____.   Page(s): _____

Fir Tree's leaves _____.   Page(s): _____

What does Fir Tree learn?

Text Evidence 🔍

At first, Fir Tree complains _____.   Page(s): _____

Fir tree helps Squirrel because _____.   Page(s): _____

Fir Tree learns _____.   Page(s): _____

Group Discussion Present your answers to the group. Cite
text evidence to justify your thinking. Listen to and discuss
the group's opinions about your answers.

Write Review your notes. Then write your answer to the
Essential Question. Use text evidence to support your answer.
Use vocabulary words in your writing.

How does Fir Tree develop differently from his friends?

In the fall, Maple, Oak, and Elm's leaves _____

_____.

Fir Tree's leaves _____.

In the winter, _____

_____.

Fir Tree learns _____

_____.

Share Writing Present your writing to the class. Discuss their
opinions. Think about what the class has to say. Do they justify
their claims? Explain why you agree or disagree.

I agree with _____ because _____. I disagree because _____.

Write to Sources

pages 352–355

Andre

Take Notes About the Text I took notes to respond to the prompt: *Mother Nature does not tell Fir Tree his purpose. In your opinion, is it better for Fir Tree to learn it by himself? Use reasons in your claim.*

Fir Tree	Maple, Oak, and Elm
In fall, leaves stay green. He complains to Mother Nature.	In fall, leaves turn beautiful shades of color.
Fir Tree keeps his leaves, but he wants to change like his friends.	Lose their leaves.
He learns his purpose is to give animals shelter.	Trees cannot give shelter to animals in the cold.

Write About the Text I used my notes to write an opinion about the myth.

Student Model: *Opinion*

It was better for Fir Tree to learn his purpose by himself. He also learned to be proud of being different. During winter, Squirrel was cold. None of the trees had leaves to keep her warm. But Fir Tree was different. Squirrel could build a nest in Fir Tree's leaves. Finally, Fir Tree understood his purpose. This made him happy to be different and proud of his leaves.

TALK ABOUT IT

Text Evidence **Circle** what Squirrel could do in winter. How did this help Fir Tree understand his purpose?

Grammar **Underline** the third sentence. How can you add the word "bitterly" to make it more descriptive?

Connect Ideas **Box** the first two sentences. How can you combine them using the word *because*?

Your Turn

What tree would you prefer to be? Give reasons for your claim.

>> *Go Digital*
Write your response online. Use your editing checklist.

359

TALK ABOUT IT

Weekly Concept We Need Energy

? **Essential Question**
How do we use energy?

>> *Go Digital*

COLLABORATE

How does the boy use energy to find information? How do you use energy? Write your ideas on the web.

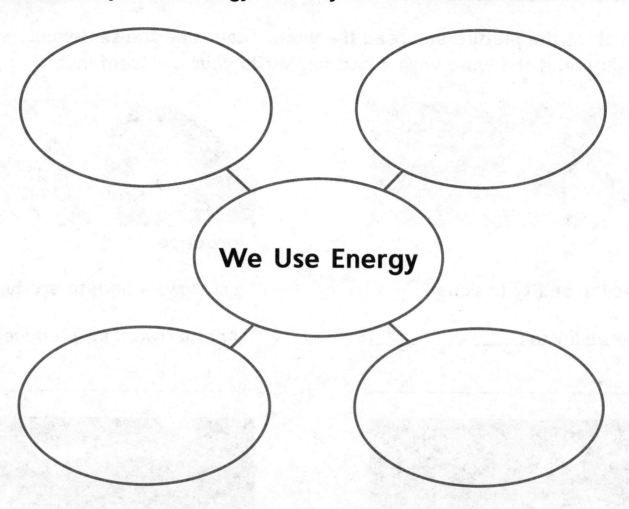

We Use Energy

Discuss ways that you use energy. Name some of the things you use that need energy to work. Use the words from the web. You can say:

I use energy to _____

_____ .

More Vocabulary

COLLABORATE

Look at the picture and read the word. Then read the sentence. Talk about the word with a partner. Write your own sentence.

ability

Victor has the **ability** to skate.

I have the *ability* to _____

_____.

pedal

I **pedal** my bike.

You *pedal* with your _____.

produce

Liz blows a horn to **produce** music.

Another word for *produce* is

_____.

rear

The horse kicked its **rear** legs.

A word that means the opposite of

rear is _____.

stored

We **stored** the food in jars.

I *stored* my clothes in _____

_____.

transferred

Ink is **transferred** from pen to paper.

When something is *transferred,* it

_____.

Words and Phrases
in place and *right away*

in place = in the same position
We ran <u>in place</u> to warm up.

right away = immediately
Your food will be ready <u>right away</u>.

Read each sentence. Write the phrase that means the same as the underlined words.

Class will start <u>immediately</u>.

Class will start _____.

The band stopped and marched <u>in the same position</u>.

The band stopped and marched _____

_____.

>> Go Digital Add *in place* and *right away* to your New Words notebook. Write a sentence to show the meaning of each phrase.

(t)©Gaetano/Corbis; (b)Matthias Hauser/imageBROKER/Getty Images

COLLABORATE

❶ Talk About It

Look at the photograph. Read the title. Talk about what you see. Write your ideas.

What does the title tell you?

_____

_____

_____.

What are the people doing?

_____

_____.

Take notes as you read the text.

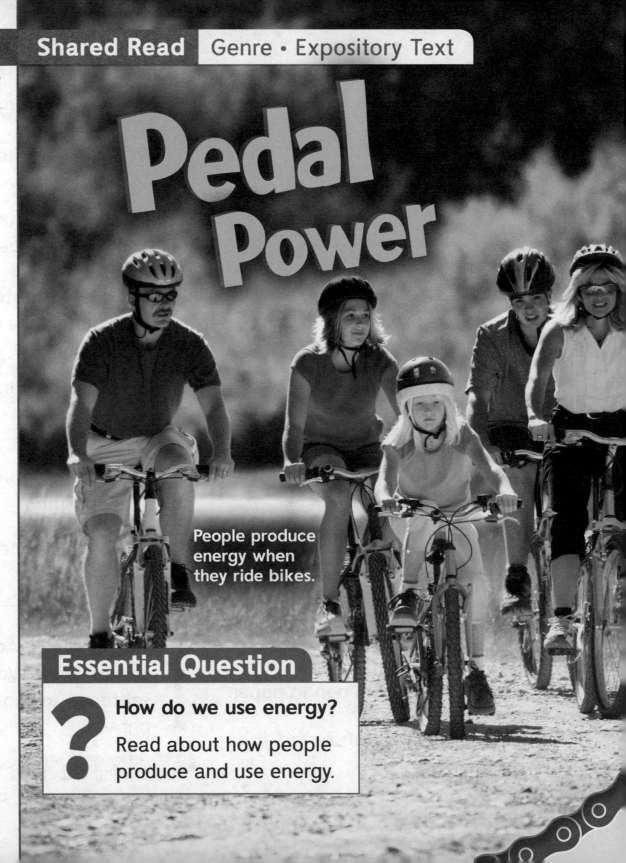

Pedal Power

People produce energy when they ride bikes.

Essential Question

? **How do we use energy?**

Read about how people produce and use energy.

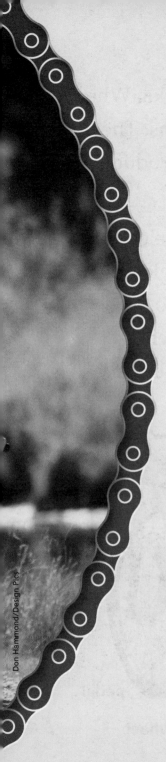

Don Hammond/Design Pics

What Is Energy?

Energy is the **ability** to do work. Solar energy comes from the Sun. It's a **silent** source of energy, because it makes no sound. There is also energy that comes from wind and water.

Did you know that energy can come from people, too? When you **pedal** a bike, you **produce** energy. You use your legs to push the pedals. Your energy is **transferred** to the bike. This shift of power or energy makes the bike move.

Now imagine riding your bike to create enough power to run a computer. Some students at one school did just that! They hopped on bikes connected to generators and pedaled in place. Soon they were producing electricity. This energy is needed to run their laptop computers.

Text Evidence

❶ Specific Vocabulary Ⓐ Ⓒ Ⓣ

Reread the first paragraph. Circle the context clue for the word *silent*. Box an example of a silent source of energy.

❷ Comprehension
Author's Purpose

Reread the second paragraph. What happens when energy produced from pedaling is transferred to the bike?

The author explains that this

_____

_____.

❸ Sentence Structure Ⓐ Ⓒ Ⓣ

Reread the last paragraph. In the third sentence, circle the words that describe the bikes students pedaled. What did pedaling these bikes produce?

_____.

365

1 Comprehension

Author's Purpose

Reread the first paragraph. Circle what makes the generator produce electricity. What does the author explain in the text?

The author explains _____

_____

_____ .

2 Specific Vocabulary ACT

The phrase *as long as* in the text means "when." Underline what happens as long as a student pedals the bicycle.

COLLABORATE

3 Talk About It

Use the diagram to explain how a bicycle generator works. What part stores energy to be used later?

Bicycle-Powered Energy

Here's how bicycle-powered energy works. When a student pedals the bike, the **rear** wheel spins. The wheel spins the generator. The generator produces electricity.

As long as a student pedals the bicycle, electricity flows, or runs, through the generator. The electricity can be used right away. This energy can also be **stored** in a battery. It can be used later. Teachers can haul, or carry, laptop computers to the battery and plug them in for power.

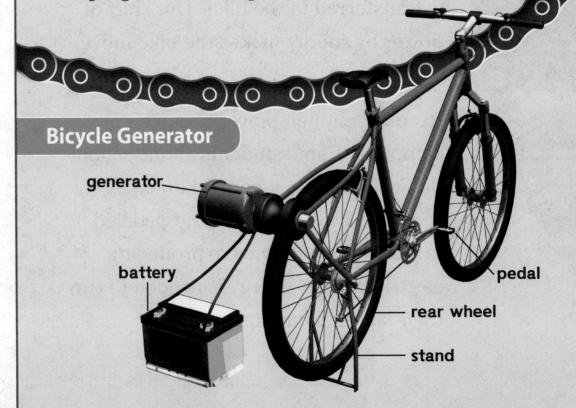

Bicycle Generator

generator

battery

pedal

rear wheel

stand

Steve Schell

Using Bicycle-Powered Energy

People also exercise on bicycles and produce power in gyms. People create watts as they pedal. A watt is a unit for measuring power. Small devices, such as small televisions and fans, often use less than 100 watts per hour. These things can be run by bicycle-powered electricity.

It would be a mistake to use pedal power to run a refrigerator, though. This large **appliance** often uses more than 700 watts per hour. The electricity for these machines comes from power lines overhead or underground.

Pedal power is popping up in schools, gyms, and homes. What a fun way to provide electricity!

Bicycle power can be used to power these appliances.

Make Connections

? How can people use the electricity they produce from riding bikes? ESSENTIAL QUESTION

Tell about how you might use bike-powered electricity. TEXT TO SELF

Text Evidence

1 Sentence Structure ⒶⒸⓉ

Reread the first paragraph. Circle the examples of small devices between the two commas.

2 Specific Vocabulary ⒶⒸⓉ

An *appliance* is a machine used in people's homes. Box the example of a large appliance in the second paragraph. Circle where electricity comes from for large appliances.

COLLABORATE

3 Talk About It

Discuss the things pedal power could run in a home. List some of these devices.

_____

_____

Respond to the Text

Partner Discussion Answer the questions. Discuss what you learned about "Pedal Power." Write the page numbers where you found text evidence.

How does bicycle-powered energy work?

Text Evidence 🔍

Pedaling causes the rear wheel _____.   Page(s): _____

The generator _____.   Page(s): _____

As long as someone pedals the bike, _____.   Page(s): _____

How can people use the energy produced by a bike?

Text Evidence 🔍

The electricity can be stored _____.   Page(s): _____

Laptop computers can _____.   Page(s): _____

Bike-powered energy can also run _____.   Page(s): _____

Group Discussion Present your answers to the group. Cite text evidence to justify your thinking. Listen to and discuss the group's opinions about your answers.

Write Review your notes about "Pedal Power." Then write your answer to the Essential Question. Use text evidence to support your answer. Use vocabulary words in your writing.

How can people produce and use energy from a bike?

Bikes were connected _____.

Students pedaled to _____

_____. The electricity was needed to run

_____ or it could be

_____. Devices that can run on pedal power are

_____

_____.

Share Writing Present your writing to the class. Discuss their opinions. Think about what the class has to say. Do they justify their claims? Explain why you agree or disagree with their claims.

I agree with _____ because _____. I disagree because _____.

369

Write to Sources

pages 364–367

Take Notes About the Text I took notes on the chart to respond to the prompt: *People can make bicycle-powered energy. Explain how this energy can be used. Use text evidence in your answer.*

Héctor

Students in a school made electricity to run laptop computers.

Uses for bicycle-powered energy

People in gyms exercise on bicycles to run small devices.

Large appliances must get electricity from power lines.

Eclipse Studios/McGraw-Hill Education

Write About the Text I used my notes to write about bicycle-powered energy.

Student Model: *Informative Text*

Bicycle-powered energy can be used to power devices. Students in school pedaled bikes connected to generators. They pedaled the bikes to produce electricity. It ran their computers. People in gyms exercise on bikes. They can make electricity to run small televisions and fans. This will not work on a refrigerator. A refrigerator needs too much power. It gets power from power lines.

TALK ABOUT IT

COLLABORATE

Text Evidence **Circle** the detail about pedal power in gyms. What examples of small devices does Héctor include?

Grammar **Underline** the first sentence that tells what kids pedaled. How can you add the word *a* to the sentence?

Condense Ideas **Box** the third and fourth sentences. How can you combine them to condense the ideas.

Your Turn

COLLABORATE

Tell why the author wrote "Pedal Power." Cite text evidence.

>> Go Digital
Write your response online. Use your editing checklist.

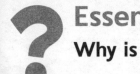

Essential Question

Why is teamwork important?

>> *Go Digital*

COLLABORATE How are the bikers exploring nature? How does teamwork help them travel and stay safe? What are other examples of teamwork? Write down your ideas.

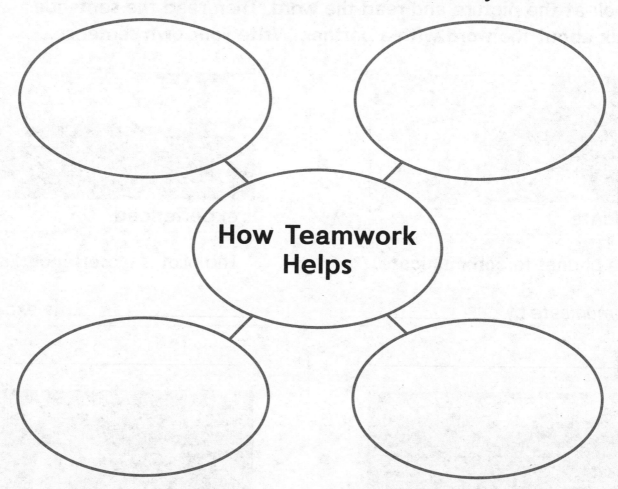

How Teamwork Helps

Discuss why teamwork is important. Use the words from the web. You can say:

Teamwork is important because _____

_____.

More Vocabulary

 Look at the picture and read the word. Then read the sentence. Talk about the word with a partner. Write your own sentence.

communicate

People use phones to **communicate**.

Dogs *communicate* by _____

_____.

diver

The **diver** swims under the water.

A *diver* may see _____

_____.

experienced

The pilot is **experienced** at flying.

_____ is *experienced* at

_____.

expert

Mr. Donaldson is a computer **expert**.

I want to be an *expert* at _____

_____.

gear

Firefighters wear special **gear**.

I wear *gear* when I _____

_____.

tasks

Washing dishes is one of my **tasks**.

Another word for *tasks* is

_____.

Words and Phrases
Adjectives *serious* and *special*

The word *serious* can mean "important."
Doctors have a <u>serious</u> job.

The word *special* can tell about
something used for a purpose.
I wear <u>special</u> shoes for dance class.

**Write *special* or *serious* to complete each
sentence.**

Cleo used a _____ tool

to fix her watch.

Police officers have a _____

job because they help people.

>> *Go Digital* **Add these meanings of the
words *serious* and *special* to your New
Words notebook. Write a sentence to
show each meaning.**

COLLABORATE

❶ Talk About It

Look at the photograph. Read the title. Talk about what you see. Write your ideas.

What does the title tell you?

_____

_____

_____.

What is the woman in the photograph doing?

_____

_____

_____.

Take notes as you read the text.

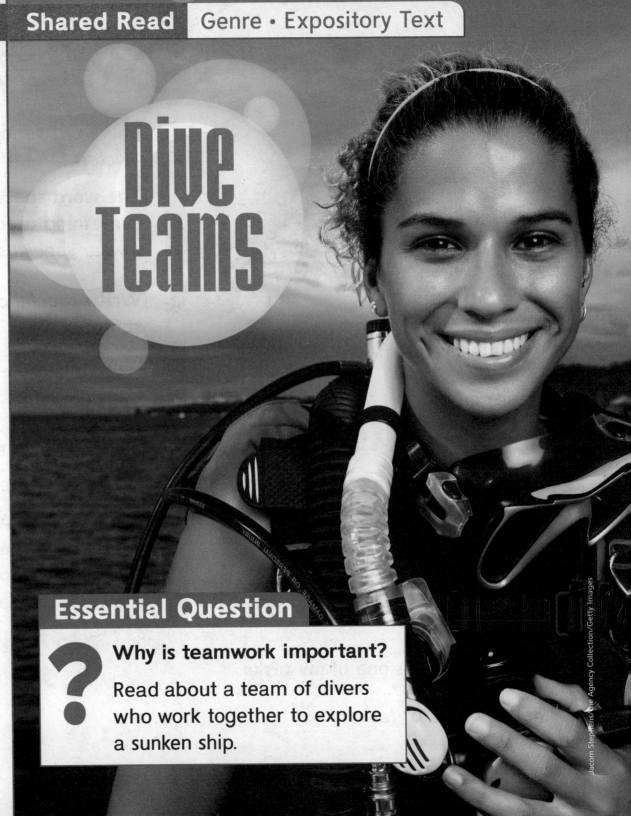

Dive Teams

Essential Question

?

Why is teamwork important?

Read about a team of divers who work together to explore a sunken ship.

Jacom Stephens/The Agency Collection/Getty Images

Imagine exploring the underwater world of the ocean. Perhaps you want to see how sea animals live, or you may hope to search for **sunken ships**. That is just what Gloria did!

Gloria has always lived close to the sea in California. She swam and surfed at an early age. She became interested in the ocean. So Gloria became an **expert diver**. She decided to join a dive team to find sunken ships. What would her job be?

Each job on a dive team is important. One serious job is using machines the dive team needs. Another job is to repair, or fix, these devices when they don't work. Gloria is an **experienced** photographer, so she decides to photograph what the team discovers underwater.

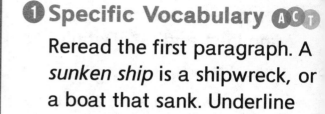

Gloria and her team search for the sunken ship.

(b) Gary Doak/Alamy

❶ **Specific Vocabulary** Ⓐ ⒸⓉ

Reread the first paragraph. A *sunken ship* is a shipwreck, or a boat that sank. Underline where someone explores to search for sunken ships.

❷ **Comprehension**

Main Idea and Key Details

Reread the third paragraph. Underline the main idea. Circle one key detail that supports this main idea.

❸ **Sentence Structure** Ⓐ ⒸⓉ

Look back at the last sentence. The word *so* connects two parts of the sentence. Underline the part that tells what Gloria does as an experienced photographer.

Text Evidence

❶ Comprehension
Main Idea and Key Details

Reread the first paragraph. Circle the main idea about dive teams. Underline how team members work together.

❷ Sentence Structure A C T

Reread the fourth sentence in the second paragraph. The word *and* separates two things, or actions, the team does. Circle the two things they do.

COLLABORATE

❸ Talk About It

On the map, circle the location of the shipwreck. At the shipwreck, what does the team do before they dive?

_____

_____ .

Teamwork is important for a dive team. Team members depend on one another. They divide up the **tasks** and each person helps to get the job done.

Gloria's team learns about a ship that sank over 100 years ago. No one has ever found it! They decide to make a scientific study of it. The team reads information and studies a map where they think the ship sank. They are excited about their exploration.

The captain, another team member, takes them by boat to their map location. He stays on the boat where he can **communicate** with the divers.

Before the team dives, they prepare for their special jobs. To get ready, Gloria puts on her diving suit and **gear** and makes sure her camera is ready to take photographs.

FLORIDA

KEY
★ Home Base
⚓ Shipwreck
- - - Route

Tallahassee
Tampa
Miami

This map shows the route Gloria's team takes to the shipwreck.

Now the divers jump into the water. As they swim deeper, it gets darker. A team member turns on a flashlight. This helps the divers see where they are going.

Finally, one team member spots the ship! He uses an aquatic microphone to talk to the team. Gloria takes pictures as teammates measure the ship. Another teammate watches for sharks and other dangers.

After an hour of exploring, the person with the flashlight leads the way back to the boat. The team now has important results from their discovery to share. Gloria thinks, "I will always remember this dive!"

The team believes the ship Gloria heard about sank near other known shipwrecks off the coast of Florida.

Make Connections

? Why is teamwork important for exploring shipwrecks? ESSENTIAL QUESTION

Would you enjoy being part of a team that explores shipwrecks? Explain your answer. TEXT TO SELF

Text Evidence

1 Comprehension
Main Idea and Key Details

Reread the first paragraph. Circle details that tell how a team member helps the other divers as they swim deeper.

COLLABORATE

2 Talk About It

Talk about the special jobs of the team members. What does one diver do to keep all the team members safe?

_____

_____

3 Sentence Structure (A)(C)(T)

Reread the first sentence in the last paragraph. A comma separates two parts of the sentence. Circle the part that tells what happens after an hour of exploring.

Respond to the Text

Partner Discussion Work with a partner. Discuss what you learned about "Dive Teams." Write the page numbers where you found text evidence.

	Text Evidence
What do the dive team members do before the dive?	
Gloria's team learns about _____.	Page(s): _____
Gloria's team studies a map _____.	Page(s): _____
To get ready, _____.	Page(s): _____

	Text Evidence
How do the teammates work together?	
As the divers swim deeper, _____.	Page(s): _____
The captain _____.	Page(s): _____
Gloria takes _____ as teammates _____.	Page(s): _____

Group Discussion Present your answers to the group. Cite text evidence to justify your thinking. Listen to and discuss the group's opinions about your answers.

Write Review your notes about "Dive Teams." Then write your answer to the Essential Question. Use text evidence to support your answer. Use vocabulary words in your writing.

Why is teamwork important for the dive team?

The dive team members divide up _____

_____.

The captain takes the divers _____.

One team member _____

as the divers swim deeper. Gloria _____

while _____.

Another teammate _____.

Share Writing Present your writing to the class. Discuss their opinions. Think about what the class has to say. Do they justify their claims? Explain why you agree or disagree with their claims.

I agree with _____ because _____. I disagree because _____.

Write to Sources

pages 376–379

Take Notes About the Text I took notes on the chart to respond to the prompt: *Did the author help you understand teamwork? Use reasons to support your claim.*

Melissa

The captain communicates with the divers.

One member uses a flashlight to help the divers see.

Team members divide up the tasks to get the job done.

One job is to repair devices the divers need.

One team member watches for dangers.

382

Write About the Text I used my notes to write my opinion about "Dive Teams."

Student Model: *Opinion*

The author helped me understand teamwork. I learned that people on a dive team each have a job. Team members keep each other safe. The captain drives the boat and communicates with the divers. One member uses a flashlight. This helps the divers see as they swim deeper. Another serious job is to watch for dangers. Teamwork means working together to get the job done.

TALK ABOUT IT

Text Evidence **Draw a box** around the sentence about the captain. How does this detail support Melissa's opinion?

Grammar **Underline** the second sentence. How can you add the adjective *special* to the sentence to tell about a job?

Condense Ideas **Circle** the sentences about the member with a flashlight. How can you combine the sentences to condense the ideas?

Your Turn

Would you like to be on a dive team? Tell why or why not. Use details from the text in your answer.

>> Go Digital
Write your response online. Use your editing checklist.

TALK ABOUT IT

Weekly Concept Money Matters

? Essential Question

How do we use money?

>> *Go Digital*

COLLABORATE

How do you think the girl will use her money? What goods, or things, and services does your family spend money on? Write your ideas on the chart.

Goods	Services

Discuss how your family uses money to buy good and services. Use the words from the chart. You can say:

My family uses money to buy goods, such as _____

_____. My family uses money to pay for services,

such as _____.

More Vocabulary

 Look at the picture and read the word. Then read the sentence.

Talk about the word with a partner. Write your own sentence.

bank

We save money in a **bank**.

People go to the *bank* to _____

_____.

exchanges

David **exchanges** money for a drink.

Another word for *exchanges* is

_____.

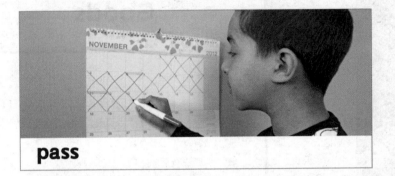

pass

A year will **pass** before his next birthday.

_____ days will *pass* before it is Saturday.

printed

Books are **printed** with this machine.

I have *printed* _____

_____.

replace

Mr. Smith will **replace** the flat tire.

We *replace* _____ when

_____ .

returned

I **returned** my books to the library.

People *return* clothing to a store if

_____ .

Words and Phrases
keep track of and *travel on*

keep track of = to write down information
I <u>keep track of</u> my team's scores.

travel on = continue to go to other places
The circus comes to town and then <u>travels on</u>.

Write the phrase that best replaces the underlined words.

I <u>write down</u> my homework assignments in a notebook.

I _____ my homework assignments in a notebook.

The bird lands in the tree and then <u>continues to go to other places</u>.

The bird lands in the tree and then _____

_____ .

>> Go Digital Add *keep track of* and *travel on* to your New Words notebook. Write sentences to show their meanings.

(t)Colleen Butler/E+/Getty Images; (b)Andersen Ross/Photodisc/Superstock

COLLABORATE

1 Talk About It

Look at the photo. Read the title. Talk about what you see. Write your ideas.

What does the title tell you?

_____

_____

_____

_____.

What do you see in the photograph?

_____

_____

_____.

Take notes as you read the text.

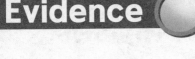

The Life of a Dollar Bill

Essential Question

? **How do we use money?**

Read to learn about how a dollar bill circulates.

(t) Kevin Zimmer; (c) Jacobs Stock Photography/Digital Vision/Getty Images

The Dollar Bill Is Printed

One day, a dollar bill is **printed** at the United States Bureau of Engraving and Printing. The bill is printed on a machine that was invented, or created, to save time. It prints many bills at a time.

The U.S. Bureau of Engraving and Printing prints bills each day.

Let's follow the dollar bill. It gets sent to a big **bank** and then a **local** bank. A family visits this neighborhood bank to get money. The dollar bill goes to a boy for his allowance.

The boy brings the dollar bill to the bookstore. He checks prices to see how much the books cost. Then he decides what he can purchase. He finds a book to buy, but is it worth the price? He's not sure. The boy reads the back of the book and thinks about the price. The boy decides the book is a good value, so he **exchanges** his money for the book.

Text Evidence

1 Specific Vocabulary (A)(C)(T)

Reread the second paragraph. Circle the word that helps you understand the meaning of *local*. Why does the family visit the local bank?

_____

_____

_____.

2 Sentence Structure (A)(C)(T)

Reread the last paragraph. The word *but* connects two parts of the fourth sentence. Circle the part that tells the boy's question about the book he finds.

3 Comprehension

Underline what the boy does to decide the book is a good value.

❶ Sentence Structure ⒶⒸⓉ

Reread the first paragraph. The word *and* connects two actions, or things, the girl does with the dollar bill. Circle what she does with the bill when she is home.

❷ Comprehension

Problem and Solution

Reread the last paragraph. The dollar bill is worn out and torn. Circle why this is a problem. Underline how the man solves his problem.

COLLABORATE

❸ Talk About It

Look back at the graph. What is the average life span of a dollar bill? When does the dollar bill in the text become worn out and torn?

The Dollar Bill Travels

Later, a girl buys a birthday card at the bookstore. She gets the dollar bill as change. She takes the dollar bill home and saves it in her piggy bank.

When the girl wants to see a movie, she takes money out of her piggy bank, including the dollar bill. She uses it to pay for the ticket. Then the dollar bill travels on.

Almost two years **pass** and now a man gets the dollar bill. It is worn out and torn. The man is not sure if it's usable. What happens to the ripped bill? The man takes it to his local bank and trades it in for a new dollar bill.

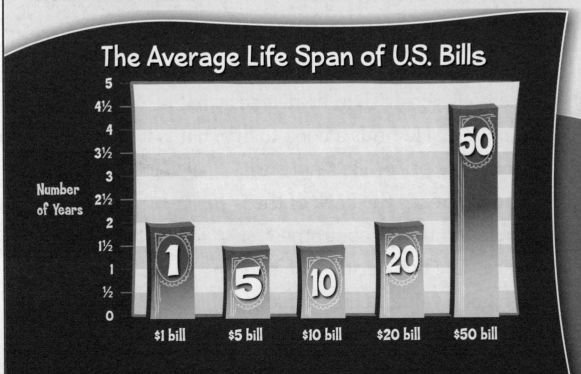

The Average Life Span of U.S. Bills

The Dollar Bill Is Replaced

The old dollar bill is **returned** to the big bank where workers decide that it can't be used again. They destroy the bill by **shredding** it. They cut it into tiny pieces.

A machine shreds over 6 billion worn-out bills a year.

Back at the U.S. Bureau of Engraving and Printing, a new dollar bill is printed to **replace** the old one. Workers use a record to keep track of how many bills are printed and destroyed. They make sure there are enough bills in the system so people can buy and sell things.

The next time you hold a one-dollar bill, think of where it has been and where it is going. Each dollar bill has a busy, useful life.

Make Connections

? Why is a dollar bill important?
ESSENTIAL QUESTION

What can you do with a one-dollar bill? TEXT TO SELF

Text Evidence

❶ Specific Vocabulary Ⓐ Ⓒ Ⓣ

Reread the first paragraph. Circle the paragraph clue to the meaning of *shredding*. Underline why the big bank decides to shred the bill.

❷ Comprehension
Problem and Solution

Reread the first sentence in the second paragraph. What is done to replace the destroyed dollar bill?

_____

_____

❸ Sentence Structure Ⓐ Ⓒ Ⓣ

Reread the last sentence in the second paragraph. The word *so* connects two parts of the sentence. Circle the part that tells why workers make sure there are enough bills in the system.

391

Respond to the Text

Partner Discussion Answer the questions. Discuss what you learned about "The Life of a Dollar Bill." Write the page numbers where you found text evidence.

Where does the dollar bill travel after it is printed?

Text Evidence

The new dollar bill gets sent _____.

Page(s): _____

The boy uses it to _____.

Page(s): _____

The girl gets it when _____ and uses it to _____.

Page(s): _____

What happens to the dollar bill when it is old?

Text Evidence

The man trades the dollar bill _____.

Page(s): _____

It is returned to the big bank where _____.

Page(s): _____

A new dollar bill _____.

Page(s): _____

Group Discussion Present your answers to the group. Cite text evidence to justify your thinking. Listen to and discuss the group's opinions about your answers.

COLLABORATE

Write Review your notes about "The Life of a Dollar Bill." Then write your answer to the Essential Question. Use text evidence to support your answer. Use vocabulary words in your writing.

What are ways people use the dollar bill?

The family _____

_____.

The girl _____

_____.

When a dollar bill is old and worn, _____

_____.

COLLABORATE

Share Writing Present your writing to the class. Discuss their opinions. Think about what the class has to say. Do they justify their claims? Explain why you agree or disagree.

I agree with _____ because _____.

I disagree because _____.

Write to Sources

Farah

Take Notes About the Text I took notes to respond to the prompt: *What does the author describe about a dollar bill? Use text evidence in your answer.*

pages 388–391

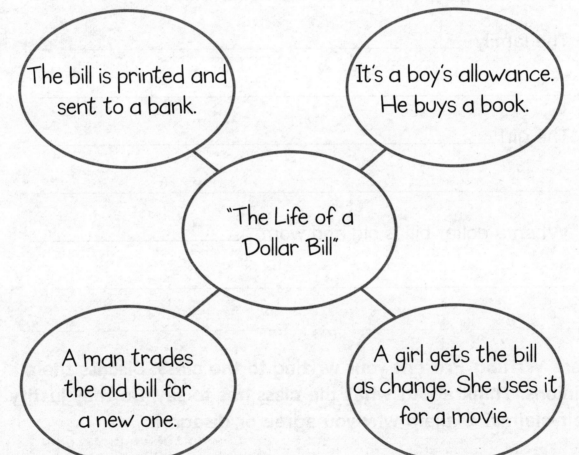

The bill is printed and sent to a bank.

It's a boy's allowance. He buys a book.

"The Life of a Dollar Bill"

A man trades the old bill for a new one.

A girl gets the bill as change. She uses it for a movie.

Write About the Text I used my notes to write about the life of a dollar bill.

The author describes where a dollar bill travels. The bill is printed and sent to a bank. A family gives it to their son for an allowance. The boy uses it to buy a book. Then, a girl receives the bill as change from the bookstore. After two years, the bill is ripped. A man trades it in, and a new dollar bill is printed to replace it.

TALK ABOUT IT

Text Evidence **Circle** the sentence that tells the end of the bill's life. How does this detail help explain why money is printed?

Grammar **Underline** the second sentence. How can you add the word *local* to describe where the bill is sent?

Connect Ideas **Box** the sentences about the boy. How can you combine the sentences to connect the ideas?

Your Turn

Why is a dollar bill important? Use text evidence to support your answer.

>> Go Digital
Write your response online. Use your editing checklist.

? **Essential Question**
Where can your imagination take you?

>> *Go Digital*

COLLABORATE

What can the girl do in her imagination? What do you like to imagine that you can do? Write your ideas on the web.

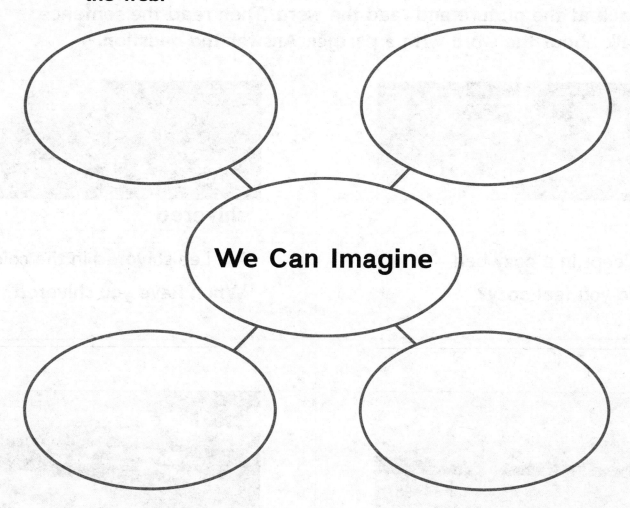

We Can Imagine

Discuss what you like to imagine that you can do or be.
Use the words from the web. You can say:

I like to imagine that I can _____.

COLLABORATE Look at the picture and read the word. Then read the sentence. Talk about the word with a partner. Answer the question.

cozy

My dog sleeps in a **cozy** bed.

Where do you feel cozy?

_____

shivered

Mr. Lee **shivered** in the cold.

When have you shivered?

_____

dreary

The weather is gray and **dreary**.

A word that means the opposite

of *dreary* **is** _____.

silky

This fabric feels **silky**.

What things are silky?

_____

Poetry Terms

message

The **message** is the big idea in a poem. It is what the poem tells readers.

The message of "The Ticket" is to use your imagination.

metaphor

A **metaphor** compares two things that are not alike.

The **box of crayons** is the **sun**.

rhyme

The words *cat* and *mat* **rhyme**. They end in the same sound.

We have a cat.
It sat on a mat.

COLLABORATE

Work with a partner. Use these words to make up a metaphor and a rhyme. Say them aloud.

whale   **king**

lion   **tail**

Metaphor:

A _____ is

the _____ of the

animal kingdom.

Rhyme:

A big _____

has a long _____.

399

❶ Literary Elements

Metaphor

Reread line one. Circle the two things the author compares in a metaphor.

❷ Specific Vocabulary ᴬᶜᵀ

Reread lines seven and eight. A *marching band* plays music and walks together. Box what the author draws to play in a marching band.

❸ Literary Elements

Message

Reread the last two lines of the poem. What can you always create with crayons?

_____

_____

_____.

A Box of Crayons

A box of crayons is the sun
on a **dreary**, rainy day.
You can draw a hot air balloon
and travel far far away.

You can draw a beach
and play in the **silky** sand.
You can draw a drum
and play in a **marching band**.

With crayons you can always create
something exciting, something great!

— by Isaiah Nowels

Essential Question

Where can your imagination take you?

Read how poems share ideas and creativity.

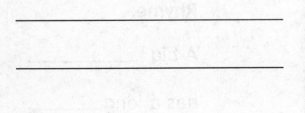

What Story Is This?

None of us are us today,
We're putting on a play.

"**Knock**, knock, knock! Someone's there!"
That's the wolf, my friend Claire.

"Not by the hair of my chinny-chin chin!"
Julie, a little pig, says with a grin.

Joseph and Pat are pigs as well.
They run to Claire's house and ring the bell.
Do you remember this story's name?

If so, you've won this guessing game!

— by Trevor Reynolds

❶ Comprehension
Point of View

Reread lines one and two. Underline what the author, or speaker, tells us about putting on a play.

❷ Specific Vocabulary Ⓐ Ⓒ Ⓣ

Reread lines three and four. When you *knock* on a door, you make a noise to tell someone you're there. Circle the character who is there.

COLLABORATE

❸ Talk About It

Reread the last two lines. Underline the question the author asks. What is the story's name?

_____

401

1 Literary Elements

Message

Look back at the first four lines of the poem. What does the author want you to know about the special ticket?

_____

_____

_____.

2 Literary Elements

Rhyme

Reread the next four lines. Circle two lines that rhyme.

3 Comprehension

Point of View

Reread the next four lines. Underline the reason the author says she "shivered in the North Pole." Circle the description of what she builds.

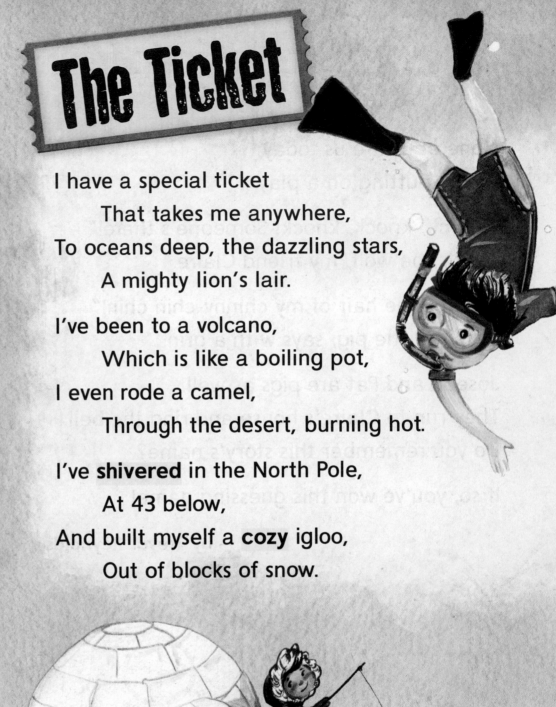

The Ticket

I have a special ticket
 That takes me anywhere,
To oceans deep, the dazzling stars,
 A mighty lion's lair.

I've been to a volcano,
 Which is like a boiling pot,
I even rode a camel,
 Through the desert, burning hot.

I've **shivered** in the North Pole,
 At 43 below,
And built myself a **cozy** igloo,
 Out of blocks of snow.

I've met a great inventor,
     And helped him to create,
A baseball playing **robot**,
     That slides into home plate.

My journeys take just seconds,
     I simply close my eyes,
And I'm a rocket sleek and silver,
     Speeding through the skies.

What's that? You'd like to join me?
     Here's all you have to do:
Use your imagination,
     And you'll soon go places, too!

— **by Constance Keremes**

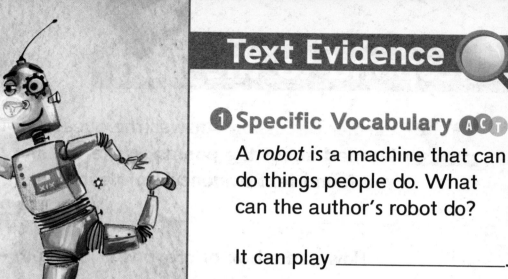

Make Connections

? Where does each poet go in his or her imagination? ESSENTIAL QUESTION

Which poem reminds you of somewhere you have been in your own imagination? TEXT TO SELF

Text Evidence 🔍

❶ Specific Vocabulary **ACT**

A *robot* is a machine that can do things people do. What can the author's robot do?

It can play _____.

COLLABORATE

❷ Talk About It

What is the author when she speeds through the skies on her journeys?

❸ Literary Elements
Message

Reread the last four lines. Circle how readers can join the author. What is the message about using your imagination?

_____

_____

Cat Zaza

Respond to the Text

Partner Discussion Answer the questions. Discuss what you learned about the poems. Write the line numbers where you found text evidence from each poem.

How can a box of crayons or being in a play help you use your imagination?	**Text Evidence**
With a box of crayons, you can _____.	Line(s): _____
You can draw _____.	Line(s): _____
When putting on a play, _____.	Line(s): _____

What does the author imagine in "The Ticket"?	**Text Evidence**
The author can go anywhere, such as _____.	Line(s): _____
She has been to _____.	Line(s): _____
She has met an inventor and _____.	Line(s): _____

Group Discussion Present your answers to the group. Cite text evidence to justify your thinking. Listen to and discuss the group's opinions about your answers.

COLLABORATE

Write Review your notes about the poems. Then write your answer to the Essential Question. Use text evidence to support your answer. Use vocabulary words in your writing.

How does the author of "A Box of Crayons" use imagination?

The author says a box of crayons is _____ on a

_____. He can draw

_____ and _____.

He can draw _____ and _____

_____.

The author tells readers that they can always create _____

_____.

COLLABORATE

Share Writing Present your writing to the class. Discuss their opinions. Think about what the class has to say. Do they justify their claims? Explain why you agree or disagree.

I agree with _____ because _____. I disagree because _____.

Write to Sources

Thomas

Take Notes About the Text I took notes on the chart to respond to the prompt: *What is the message in the poem "A Box of Crayons"?* Use text evidence in your answer.

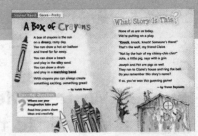

pages 400–403

A box of crayons is the sun on a rainy day.

You can draw a hot air balloon and travel far away.

Message in the Poem "A Box of Crayons"

You can draw a drum and play in a marching band.

You can draw a beach and play in the sand.

Write About the Text I used my notes to write about the author's message.

In "A Box of Crayons," the author shares a message about using your imagination. The author explains how you can draw something "exciting." The author says you can draw a hot air balloon. You can travel far away. The author writes that you can draw a beach and play in the sand. The author thinks a box of crayons is the sun on a rainy day. It allows you to use your imagination and have fun.

TALK ABOUT IT

COLLABORATE

Text Evidence Circle the sentence about the beach. Why does Thomas use this detail to explain the poem's message?

Grammar Underline the sentence about a box of crayons on a rainy day. How can you add the word *dreary* to the sentence?

Condense Ideas Box the third and fourth sentences. How can you combine these sentences?

Your Turn

COLLABORATE

What is the message in the poem "The Ticket"? Use text evidence in your answer.

>> *Go Digital*
Write your response online. Use your editing checklist.

407